SHADES
OF
INNOCENCE

Other titles by Carroll Multz

The Devil's Scribe—Nadine Siena has risen from her humble beginnings as an orphan to earn the Pulitzer Prize for journalism. When an anonymous source contacts her with a story lead, she gets embroiled in a scandal that has already cost one life and threatens to bring the town of Pembrooke to its knees. As Siena fights to protect her source, a journalist from the rival newspaper begins a treacherous campaign that threatens to destroy Nadine's career and the newspaper for which she works. As the situation quickly unravels and the attorneys face off, no one can believe the final outcome or the swift, sure destructive power of the pen.

The Chameleon— The Chameleon is an undercover cop and master of deception. As he lives and works in the world of illusion, he neglects the real world and the family that finally gives up on him. When he realizes what he has sacrificed, he is determined not to blow his second chance at love and happiness. Meanwhile, he continues to try and solve the execution-style slaying of his father, a former FBI agent. His hopes begin to fade when he discovers the woman he loves is connected to an underworld kingpin. As everything unravels and he is plunged deeper into danger and darkness he also learns this man is perhaps the very person responsible for his father's death. The Chameleon must play the role of a lifetime so he can finally step out of the shadows.

License to Convict—Morrey Dexter wasn't used to losing. As a district attorney in Paraiso County, Colorado, Morrey owned the courtroom. He was dauntless in his quest to seek justice, committed to his sense of fairness, and vigilant in his role as a protector of the community. But, when a surprising verdict shakes his faith in the system, he begins to see that things are not as simple as they appear. Can Morrey use his license to convict to preserve the things he holds sacred?

Deadly Deception–Everywhere he looks, Harvard grad and former golden boy Drew Quinlin from the district attorney's office sees Joy's piercing turquoise eyes. He tries to end their affair and things spin wildly out of control. There is a horrible accident and Joy is dead. Now Drew Quinlin is drawn into the biggest case of his career, defending the person charged with her death–her husband. Will winning an acquittal appease his tortured conscience or will judgment come before he can atone for his crime?

Justice Denied–Max has come home to help. His father, Jamie Cooper, a devoted dad and faithful employee is accused of stealing $30,000 from the bank for which he worked. He hires a defense team and fights to clear his name, but will that be enough to battle the combined strength of the town's powerful chief of police, a man who has held a grudge against the Cooper family for years?

SHADES
OF
INNOCENCE

Carroll Multz

BRASS FROG BOOKWORKS™
Independent Publishers
Grand Junction, CO

Scripture taken from the Holy Bible, International Version ®, NIV ®. Copyright © 1973, 1978, 1984 by International Bible Society. Used by permission of Zondervan. All rights reserved.

This is a work of fiction. The character names, places, entities and incidents are a product of the author's imagination or, if real, used fictitiously.

The opinions expressed by the author are not necessarily those of Brass Frog Bookworks™

Published by BRASS FROG BOOKWORKS™ Independent Publishers
2695 Patterson Rd. Unit 2-#168 | Grand Junction, CO 81506
909-239-0344 or 970-434-9361 | www.BrassFrogBookworks.com

Brass Frog Bookworks is dedicated to excellence and integrity in the publishing industry. The company was founded on the belief in the power of language and the spiritual essence of human creativity. *"In the beginning was the Word…"* John 1:1

Book design copyright © 2013 by Brass Frog Bookworks. All rights reserved
Cover and interior design: Laurie Goralka Design

Inquiries should be addressed to:
Carroll Multz
859 Quail Run Dr.
Grand Junction, CO 81505

Printed in the United States of America | First Printing 2013

Library of Congress Cataloging-in-Publication Data Available
ISBN: 978-0-9857191-6-6

1. Fiction/Legal 2. Fiction/Suspense3. Fiction/Romance

DEDICATION

This novel is dedicated to the loving memory of my sister,
Marilynn Jean Kuenzi

There will be signs in the sun, the moon, and the stars,
and on earth nations will be in dismay, perplexed by
the roaring of the sea and the waves. People will die
of fright in anticipation of what is coming upon the
world, for the powers of the heavens will be shaken.

Luke 21:25-26

TABLE OF CONTENTS

AUTHOR'S NOTE

There has always been a raging debate as to which of the following factors has the greatest impact upon shaping a person's life and thus his or her destiny: heredity or environment. Having been a pre-med major and later a pre-law major, I have taught college courses in biology and chemistry and still teach a course in ethics. You would think by now I could reach a definitive resolution and settle the issue once and for all, at least in my own mind. Unfortunately, I have been unable to do so.

In *Shades of Innocence*, the principal characters are identical twins. Both share virtually the same DNA and both were exposed to the same environment. Yet, despite their personal appearances, they are as different as night and day. Their philosophical differences will become apparent. The reader will observe that circumstances, real or perceived, have a great impact in shaping the destinies of Crimson and Jade. Distorted perceptions, the reader will observe, skew rationale and thus life-altering decisions. Once derailed, the ultimate question is whether the deceived can ever get back on track. Hopefully, at least that question can be answered by book's end.

This novel has been dedicated to the memory of my only sibling, my sister, Marilynn, who went to be with the Lord in the midst of my writing this novel. Even though she was younger than I, she was always an inspiration. As with Indi in the novel, I was elated when I was told I would have a baby sister. My life would never have been the same without her.

My sister spoke and taught several languages, including French. It was as a result of hers and my mother's patience that I learned the phrases that have made their cameo appearances herein. My French connection is my heritage, and my niece who lives with her family just outside Paris. Nicole, thank you for having provided me with the impetus to make Paris an integral part of my novel.

I thank Judith Blevins and Dr. Don Carpenter, both authors in their own right, for their insight and technical assistance. But for their encouragement and that of my daughters, Lisa Knudsen and Natalie Lowery, *Shades of Innocence* might have languished in my pile of unfinished works.

And, last but not least, my special thanks to my publisher Brass Frog Bookworks™ and especially my editors Patti Hoff and Jan Weeks. Having three novels at the publisher at the same time I thought would be an ordeal but, thanks to Patti and Jan, it was just the opposite. My appreciation to them always.

To my readers, be not dismayed. Each of you is still a master of your own destiny.

PART ONE

THE ELEVENTH HOUR

DEATH ROW

HOW DO YOU PROVE A NEGATIVE? How do prove you didn't do what you've been accused of doing? How persuasive is a denial?

Sitting in the courtroom during her murder prosecution and listening to her attorney's final plea to the jury was as vivid as yesterday. Pondering her fate for a crime she didn't commit always involved asking herself the same questions Cordell Desmond Whittaker had asked the obstinate jury over four years before. She was almost forty-nine then. Now, she was in the checkout lane.

Central California Women's Facility (CCWF) was a prison established in 1990 to house prisoners at all security levels in the minimum to maximum range. As a result of an executive order of Governor Pete Wilson in 1991, all female death row inmates in California are required to be housed at CCWF. It is located in Chowchilla, California, in a corridor between Fresno to the south, and Merced to the north. The impressive compound occupies six hundred and forty acres, and is served by a staff of over twelve hundred. It has a prison population of around four thousand.

The condemned housing is the exclusive domain for inmates with death sentences. There are thought to be close to one hundred female inmates awaiting execution at CCWF. Crimson Ziang was one of them.

Crimson was not at all the poster child for the condemned woman on death row. Though her exposure to the sun's rays had been sparse in recent years, her heritage had provided her with a natural healthy glow eagerly sought by the sun worshipers who adorned the sandy beaches of the Pacific. Of Chinese descent, she was uncharacteristically tall with long, shiny dark hair, usually tied into a neat pony tail. Dark, gleaming eyes peered from beneath a fringe of bangs that hung over her forehead. Crimson had a beautiful smile that revealed straight white teeth. Even the guards referred to her as *the misfit*. The aberration didn't stop there.

The Chowchilla Resort was a term coined for the special accommodations provided for the death row inmates. Unlike the two-bunk maximum security cells provided elsewhere on the prison campus, the cells on death row were slightly larger, had single occupancy, and were equipped with television sets, CD players and other amenities reminiscent of a college dormitory. Although cell phones normally were not allowed, death row inmates for the most part had liberal telephone privileges, unlike the general prison population. Reading and writing materials and certain personal memorabilia, depending upon their nature, were permitted.

The death row inmates also differed from the general prison population in regard to the frequency and type of prison visits. The condemned's visits were much more liberal and unlike visits characteristic of the general practice elsewhere in the institution. The condemned were allowed contact visits in isolation, subject only to the ever-watchful eyes of guards positioned on the other side of a Plexiglass wall.

Despite the nonpermanent nature of their stay and the improbability of reintegration into society, the condemned at CCWF were afforded academic opportunities, work and vocational training, counseling, participation in specialized training and other worthwhile programs. All-in-all, the condemned were not discriminated against because of their status. Nor were they coddled. It was undeniable, however, that the condemned were afforded more liberal privileges as their destiny drew near.

The sound of voices and boot heels on the hard concrete floor grew louder as the two men approached her cell. The sounds were stifled, as was the harsh light outside her cell, by the heavy blanket pulled over her head. She couldn't tell what time it was, only that it was early in the morning. How long the sun had been up she wouldn't have been able to tell even if her head was exposed. As she peered out from under the blanket, an imposing uniformed guard stood frowning at her. He was accompanied by a tall gangly man with a kind face.

"Rise and shine," the guard barked. His voice was raspy and impatient. "The chaplain is starting on this end of the cellblock this morning if you want to speak with him and receive communion, but you need to get a move on."

Crimson wiped sleep from her eyes and squinted at the two figures outside her cell.

"What time is it?" she asked still half asleep.

"Six forty-five," the guard replied. "Your cell is the first stop."

"Yeah, sure," Crimson said as she got up and pulled the blanket around her shoulders like a robe.

"Stand back away from the door," the guard ordered as he motioned with his hand. "Place your hands on the wall."

Crimson knew the drill. She stood facing the wall and put her hands in front of her. The keys rattled in the lock as the guard let the chaplain into her cell.

The guard locked the cell and Crimson turned to assess her visitor. The chaplain appeared to be in his late sixties or early seventies. He smiled and extended his hand.

"I'm Father Marquand."

She accepted his hand, giving it only a perfunctory shake. "I'm not Catholic," she said bluntly.

"That just means I can't give you communion," he replied as he looked for a place to sit.

"Have a seat," Crimson said as she pulled a straight-backed chair away from a battered wooden table. "I'll just sit on the edge of the bed."

Crimson felt she had had no choice but to allow Father Marquand into her cell. Now, that he was here, she felt serenity in his presence.

Father Marquand sat quietly and stared at Crimson. It made her feel uneasy and she wrung her hands in her lap.

"Why are you staring at me like that?" she finally asked.

Father Marquand just shook his head, absorbed in thought. Finally he answered. "For the last ten years I have been a chaplain at CCWF. I came here right after my retirement as a parish priest in Boston, and I've been ministering to inmates on death row for at least half that time. I must admit that you are the first death row inmate that causes me to rethink my position on the death penalty."

"I'm sure it's warranted in some circumstances," Crimson said. "There are certain crimes that, by their very nature, invite the death penalty. The death penalty serves as a way to eradicate those who pose grave risk of harm to others."

He smiled. "You sound like a judge friend I sometimes play golf with."

Crimson managed a smile of her own. "I used to be an attorney," she said, waiting for his reaction. "Not only was I an attorney, but a prosecutor." She waited for Fr. Marquand's reaction.

He gazed at her for a moment. Only a flicker of thought registered in his expression. "None of us are perfect, not even lawyers. We all make mistakes, and when we do, regardless of who we are there is a price to be paid. For some, that can be a heavy price."

"Father, the Bible says, 'If you do the deed, you should bleed!' Right?"

Father Marquand hesitated and arched his eyebrows. He nodded.

Crimson looked straight into the chaplain's eyes. Squaring her shoulders, she asked, "Is it God's way, or his will to make someone bleed when they *didn't* do the deed?"

Father Marquand didn't immediately respond. "Are you telling me you received the death penalty for something you didn't do?" he asked. The chaplain frowned and tilted his head. "If what you say is true, and since you are a lawyer, why aren't you fighting what you say is an unwarranted conviction?"

"I've been through the whole ordeal of the arrest, charge, and conviction. That was bad enough. But the post-conviction proceedings—the appeals and petitions to courts at all levels has drained me emotionally. And for what purpose? They've all been denied."

"Have you tried to obtain a stay of execution or a grant of clemency from the governor?"

"We have tried everything, all to no avail. There have been intermittent reprieves that have been granted and then almost immediately withdrawn. The resetting of the execution date over and over again is driving me mad. Getting my hopes up one day and having them dashed the next is like dying a thousand deaths. I just want it over. All I want to do is just die in peace."

"I'll help you pray for a miracle," Fr. Marquand promised as the guard announced his time was up.

"Your lawyer is here to see you," the guard announced. He unlocked the door to her cell and after placing her in shackles, led her into a secured conference room used by attorneys to confer with their clients outside the cellblocks.

"Come to say goodbye?" Crimson asked bitterly as she greeted Cordell Desmond Whittaker. Corkey, as she called him, was her former employer and the attorney who had represented her throughout the trial and post-trial phases.

He ignored her comment and arranged a sheaf of papers on the table. "Against your wishes, I have made one last plea to the governor of California for a stay," Corkey said almost apologetically.

"We both know it will be denied," Crimson said.

"How do you know?" Corkey asked.

"It's in the stars," Crimson replied.

Corkey shook his head. "That's ridiculous!"

"We'll see," Crimson said secretly hoping that Corkey was right.

"Don't forget that old saying, 'Justice is seldom denied but often delayed,'" he reminded her. "You mustn't give up hope. I haven't."

"I don't think that's quite how the saying goes."

"In your case, your innocence will ultimately set you free."

"Promise?"

"Not just a promise—a guarantee!

"I won't hold my breath," Crimson said as she was led back to her cell.

Crimson had been counting the months, weeks, days, hours and even seconds of her incarceration. There was no way of calculating her remaining time on earth. She was not eager to hasten the process, nor did she unnecessarily want to prolong the inevitable. But amidst it all, she had been able to find peace with herself, and peace with the Creator whose own son had also been wrongfully condemned.

PART TWO

THE JOURNEY BEGINS

THE FAMILY TREE

NEAR GOLDEN GATE PARK is an import shop specializing in oriental novelties. Ziang Oriental Imports was founded in 1928 by Kilin Ziang and his wife Anwei. By 1940, the obscure shop had evolved into a flourishing business reminiscent of Fifth Avenue department stores in the nation's largest city. Several satellites of ZOI would dot the landscapes of a number of other California cities by the mid-1900s.

Kilin learned the import trade from his father, Tulan, who operated several small shops in Hong Kong. Tulan married into the Yuman family which, from the beginning, had bankrolled his ventures. Much of the merchandise Tulan sold was imported from his wife's relatives who lived in Taiwan. He followed the time-honored tradition of his in-laws: buy low, sell high; buy in quantities and at distress; sell at retail with high markup; and minimize the overhead by paying low salaries and few benefits.

Before migrating to the United States, Kilin had married Anwei Ming. Also from a wealthy family, Anwei formed a formidable business partnership with Kilin that was unparalleled at the time. Anwei was a shrewd business woman and, in later years, despite the immensity of the family business and her dwindling health, she continued to be the chief financial officer.

Within two years after their arrival in the United States, Anwei had given birth to a son whom they named Lanzu. A year and a half later, Lanzu's sister, Kaitay, was born. Lanzu learned every aspect of the business. As the heir apparent to the Ziang dynasty, he was educated at the best schools. Lanzu met his future bride, Chenzoi Chian while attending the University of San Francisco. Chenzoi had the looks of a starlet and the grace of a princess. The handsome couple stood out in a crowd like two bright stars on a moonless night. Each was fascinated with the other and both were the objects of fascination by their peers.

Chenzoi was also a first generation American. Her parents had arrived from China the year before Lanzu's. Her father Dairen and her mother Suki were natives of Shanghai. Her mother's maiden name was Yen-chi. The Chians and Yen-chis were neighbors, and Dairen and Suki had grown up together. The families ran a thriving Chinese restaurant called Chi-Yen's. It was natural that Dairen and Suki be betrothed. They were married in a traditional Chinese wedding on April 6, 1927. Six months later they left China and set sail for their new home in San Francisco.

The Chians eventually established a restaurant in Chinatown bearing the name Chi-Yen Chinese-American Cuisine. Chenzoi was born in 1930, sandwiched in between a brother, Shen-lee, and a sister, Kimsu.

Chenzoi became Mrs. Lanzu Ziang on June 12, 1950. The wedding was held in a chapel located near the University of San Francisco campus. The ceremony was fairly elaborate, with a formal reception at Chi-Yen Chinese-American Cuisine. Family members from both sides of the family came from as far away as China and Taiwan. Lanzu was just twenty; Chenzoi, eighteen. Both obtained college degrees in time for the arrival of their first child, a son whom they named Indigo, but who went by the nickname Indi.

Five years later, on Memorial Day of 1958, Chenzoi gave birth to identical twin girls. Lanzu and Chenzoi named them Crimson and Jade. According to Chinese tradition, red is a symbol of fire and blood and signifies charity, bravery and courage. Green is the symbol of nature and youth and signifies the hope of eternal life. Chinese culture had traditionally held that daughters were not valued as much as sons. In China, some were even killed at birth. Many of those traditions began to change when Chinese immigrants came to the United States and gender bias was no longer as widespread as it once was. These beautiful girls were joyfully welcomed into the growing family.

Chenzoi was troubled by the fact that she could not tell her twins apart. She thought nature would have offered her some type of mark or slight difference that would allow easy identification. The problem was solved when at the age of three months the girls had small yin-yang symbols tattooed on their right ankles.

Jade's symbol had the light half on the right, and the dark half on the left. The coloring of Crimson's tattoo was just the opposite. Now their parents could tell them apart.

ZIANG FAMILY TREE
FOUR GENERATIONS

Paternal Great-grandfather
Tulan Ziang

Maternal Great-grandfather
Mandrin Chian

Paternal Grandfather
Kilin Ziang

Paternal Grandmother
Anwei Ziang (Ming)

Paternal Grandfather
Dairen Chian

Paternal Grandmother
Suki Chian (Yen-chi)

Father
Lanzu Ziang

Mother
Chenzoi Ziang (Chian)

Aunt
Kaitay Ziang

Aunt
Kimsu Chian

Uncle
Shen-lee Chian

Children
Son
Indigo (Indi) Ziang

Daughters
Crimson Ziang, Jade Ziang

PART THREE

THE GREAT MYSTERY OF LIFE

CHENZOI

FOREIGN TO THE ANCIENT RELIGION of my ancestors is the belief that the eternal destiny of every human being has been predetermined since the beginning of creation. Contrary to the teaching of my parents, I have come to believe that some human beings are predestined to goodness and happiness, others to evil and misery. The doctrine that advances this theory is called predestination. Since my college days, it has been a theory to which I subscribe.

I have been a student of the spiritual forces for as long as I can remember. Even today, I have a regimen I follow throughout the day with minimal deviation. My course of action and methodology are determined by the configurations of the stars and planets as dictated by my astrological chart. My horoscope has thus influenced my life and defined my destiny and the path I take to determine it.

I was born in San Francisco, California, on November 1, 1930. My zodiac sign using the Western horoscope, which I prefer over the Chinese horoscope, is Scorpio. The characteristics associated with that sign are secretive, intense and passionate. They describe me to a tee. There are characteristics associated with other zodiac signs that also define me: conservative, sensitive, independent, cautious, modest and practical. Lanzu proclaims my spirituality and has tried to convince me that it was no coincidence that I was born on November 1, the Christian celebration of All Saints Day.

Our son, Indigo, nicknamed Indi, was born on March 25, 1953. His astrological sign is Aries. It is providence then that he is bold, courageous and energetic. He has certainly been a blessing to the family and a source of joy to both his father and me. He had only recently quit pestering us about having a little brother or sister.

It was intended that Indi would be our only child. It was more than a surprise when I learned I was pregnant again. And needless to say, we were all stunned when we learned there would be multiple births. It had been five years since the birth of Indi and there had been no multiple births on either side of our respective families for several generations, at least none of which Lanzu and I were aware.

It was not only Indi who was excited about the prospects of having two siblings but Lanzu as well. That surprised me since both of us had come from rather small families and both of us had been indoctrinated on the merits of controlled population growth. Even so, Lanzu said he considered it to be a double blessing to have twins. Male or female; to him, it didn't make any difference.

When my obstetrician, Dr. Kim Sepate, a Vietnamese doctor of some renown, explained the twin phenomenon, both Lanzu and I marveled at the great miracle of double birth. Dr. Sepate told us to expect identical twins.

Crimson and Jade were born on May 30, 1958. Although their looks were identical, their dispositions could not have been more different. Tattooing small yin-yang emblems on the right ankle of each child allowed us to compare and contrast those mannerisms and peculiarities, and more importantly, to identify the twin to whom they applied. One child had the dark part of the pattern on the right; the other had the dark pattern on the left.

Tattooing also served a practical purpose. As it turned out, Jade was allergic to cow's milk. It was imperative, therefore, that the twin whose tattoo bore the black pattern on the right not inadvertently ingest milk products. It was not long, however, before we could identify the twins by their personalities, which were anything but identical.

I had not put much faith in the Chinese zodiac because everyone who has ever been born fits under one of the twelve signs. I have become even more cynical after reviewing the characteristics of those born in 1958 under the Chinese sign of the Dog. I do not find that all the characteristics apply to either twin and when I list them find they are contradictory.

Those reputedly born under the sign of the Dog, for example, are honest, yet often guilty of telling white lies. Also, as Crimson and Jade celebrate their third birthday, it is easy to determine that each does not possess the same characteristics. I can already predict, with a reasonable degree of certainty, which one will grow up to be loyal, faithful, honest, and sensitive and which one will grow up to be distrustful, temperamental, self-centered, manipulative, prone to mood swings and predisposed to fabrication. Don't ask me to tell you which characteristics apply to which twin.

LANZU

I WAS BORN ON JANUARY 12, 1927, also in San Francisco, California. My zodiac sign, using the Western horoscope at Chenzoi's insistence, is Capricorn. Chenzoi tells me that the characteristics associated with my astrological sign define many things about me. And well they might. I do think of myself as ambitious, cautious and practical. However, I feel there are characteristics associated with other signs that fit me as well, such as curious, independent, intelligent and diplomatic. As far as the Chinese zodiac is concerned, I was born under the sign of the Tiger. According to Chenzoi, that means I am authoritative (she accuses me of that all the time), self-possessed, courageous, warm-hearted, intense and ready to pounce at any time.

If ready to pounce at any time means that I am very protective of my family, then it is an apt description. Having a younger sister made me aware at an early age of the responsibilities that go along with being a big brother and a protector. Although Kaitay was less than two years younger than me, I felt a sense of duty and reveled in her reliance upon me. I wanted to fulfill all of her expectations and be the hero that she thought I was and what I purported to be. The same thing was true with respect to Chenzoi. She refers to me as her Prince Charming and has always depended upon my leadership, loyalty, love and imperturbability. It is a role that I accept with the humility bred in me by my ancestors.

My role as father comes with the same challenges and rewards. My son, Indi, has been nothing short of a divine gift and was barely five years old when his twin sisters were born. He is now eight. I've already begun grooming him to take over the family businesses. When I look at him, I see myself twenty-six years ago when I was his age and looking at life through different eyes. He has adjusted well to all the attention being focused on his twin sisters and is a replica of both me and his grandfather on my side of the family.

Crimson and Jade just celebrated their third birthdays. It seems like only yesterday that I witnessed them take their first breaths. They reminded me of little birds because they were so tiny and fragile and so dependent. Crimson, when she was born, weighed in at just a little over four and a half pounds. Jade was slightly heavier at four and three-quarter pounds. To the naked eye they appeared identical and you couldn't tell them apart. One, however, had a heftier set of lungs and, from the day she was born, let us know she had an attitude. The other appeared more content and not as assertive.

I was against the tattooing to begin with although I will have to admit that when the twins weren't fussing or wailing I didn't know who was who. Even with the tattooing, I had difficulty remembering which twin had what color configuration. To add to the confusion, Chenzoi made sure they were dressed the same.

To be honest, I did not expect sibling rivalry at such an early age between Crimson and Jade. I mention the twins in the order I do, not just on the basis of the order of the first letters in their names as they appear in the alphabet, but in the order in which they were born. Crimson was born a few minutes ahead of Jade. Other than that, there is no intended order of priority. In fact, I don't love one more than the other or favor, either deliberately or subconsciously, one over the other. I hope I am not perceived otherwise.

As far as appearances are concerned, Crimson and Jade are indistinguishable except maybe in the shade of the intensity of the light reflected in their eyes and occasionally the configuration of their mouths. Crimson's mouth is usually turned up, Jade's down. Also, we've noticed Jade has a chronic frown and is more withdrawn than Crimson. Jade has some troubling habits that are of concern even at this stage in her life, such as fitful demonstrations when things don't go her way. Her spirit is forceful and she shows disregard for her sister, and disrespect for her mother and me. Discipline is woefully ineffective. Even taking away her favorite toys doesn't seem to make an impression on Jade. She is defiant and invites conflict. I am frustrated by my inability to make a lasting impression and achieve conformance.

INDI

I'VE BEEN KEEPING MY THOUGHTS pretty much to myself. I am afraid to say what I think because my parents seem to take everything I say the wrong way. Like the other day, I observed Crimson being blamed for something Jade did. Jade had taken her colored markers and scribbled on the newly painted wall in the game room. When asked who did it, Jade pointed at Crimson. Crimson was sent to her room with a scolding and when she protested she was paddled. I was told to stay out of it when I tried to explain that Crimson was not involved.

I was five when my sisters were born. I had wanted a brother or sister and was excited when Crimson and Jade arrived. Nothing has been the same since and I have taken my duties as a big brother seriously. Almost overnight I went from being the center of attention to being ignored. "That is the male's role," I was told by my father. I have watched as my mother's role has also changed. She no longer seems to have much time for me as her hands are full with the twins who this past week celebrated their third birthday.

Although Crimson and Jade look alike, they are really not difficult to tell apart. I try not to have a favorite, but my heart is drawn to Crimson. Like me, she is a pleaser. She shares her toys and does not have the mean streak that I see in Jade. It is unusual for her to whine or pout when she doesn't get her way. She is maybe too accepting of her sister and too accommodating in attempting to avoid a confrontation. She is not the only one who bows to Jade's temper tantrums and ferocious outbursts. Everything is all about Jade and there is no way but her way. She accuses me of being mean to her and not liking her. She accuses our parents of the same thing. In fact, to keep the peace, my parents usually give in to her.

PART FOUR

STANDING AT
THE GATE

CRIMSON

BEING A TWIN CARRIES a celebrity status. I determined that at an early age. Because I was born first, I assume that was the reason why the Yin-Yang symbol tattooed on my right ankle bore the white pattern on the left. Because of my Chinese heritage, I am told that is the preferred pattern and the one that defines one's destiny as being bright and promising. Maybe it was something more than a coincidence that the configuration was what it is.

Today, Jade and I celebrate our thirteenth birthday. I don't know what becoming a teen means in the Chinese culture, but I know what it means in California, U.S.A. Probably in every culture it is that magical moment when a person is in transition, being neither a child nor an adult. It appears to be an era of entitlements without any responsibilities. In other words, it appears to be an age during which the benefits are meant to be enjoyed without having to worry about the detriments. The word "teen" to Jade means anger, wrath, grief and suffering and if you don't believe me ask her. According to Jade, that is one of the definitions found in *Webster's New World Dictionary*. In checking the dictionary, I find she is partially correct.

Our parents have been most creative in making our birthdays landmark events. I call them extravaganzas. This year, our parents have booked the ballroom at the Fairmont Hotel and have kept the entertainment a surprise. Not even Jade's promises and threats have been effective in prying the information from Indi. He is very closed mouth. Last year for our twelfth birthday, we were at the Mark Hopkins Hotel listening to the droning sounds of the Pantels. They were from New Zealand and a last minute replacement for the Beatles. There were over one hundred of our neighbors, classmates and friends attending the affair. The guest list this year has swelled to over one hundred and fifty, not counting parents and the usual uninvited siblings. If Jade had her way, it would be double that.

When Mum knocked on my door at seven-thirty this morning, I had already taken my shower and was drying my hair. Jade and I had stayed up late last night listening to Beatles music, brooding over their breakup. We both agreed that as a unit, the Beatles were greater than the sum of their parts. We could not agree, however, on which of their songs was the greatest. My favorite was "Yesterday"; Jade's was "Hey, Jude." She contends that they misspelled her name.

Although we have the same genes and look alike, our similarities seem to stop there. As evidenced from our inability to agree on the greatest Beatle song and my like of ballads, we have dissimilar tastes. In fact, that is an understatement. The truth of the matter is that our tastes and feelings are as different as night and day. A case in point is the assessment of our parents. I am grateful for the life provided by them and feel we are privileged. Jade, on the other hand, questions their motives, considers their provisions as entitlements and criticizes their parenting skills. She calls our parents dictators and control freaks.

Disagreeing over our taste in music and Mum and Daddy's parenting skills doesn't seem like much. And maybe it isn't. However, disagreement is a theme that has permeated our life together. That may be one of the reasons why my parents positioned our bedrooms on opposite ends of the house. Our home is an older but elegant one situated on the northwest corner of San Francisco near Golden Gate National Recreational Area. My room overlooks South Bay and the Pacific Ocean; Jade's overlooks Alcatraz Island in San Francisco Bay. Even though the former federal prison has been closed for a number of years, Jade boasts that someday she will be housed there.

Our home is located on the same end of town as Chinatown where Chi-Yen Chinese-American Cuisine, our family restaurant, has been located now for over forty years. It is near Nob Hill where the Mark Hopkins Hotel is located and where our birthday party this year will be held. San Francisco is one of the most fascinating cities in the world and, as far as I am concerned, has lived up to its reputation as America's favorite city. It has a large oriental population, including a number of Chinese descent. This may be the main reason why my grandparents on both sides of the family settled here. I would not want to live anywhere else in the world. This may be the only thing that Jade and I agree upon.

As I put the finishing touches on my hair, Jade enters my room. "I can't find my earrings with the emerald stones Dad gave me." She frowns at me, her eyes narrowed.

"I didn't take them," I say. It is obvious she doesn't believe me as she rifles through my jewelry box anyway.

Spotting the earrings I received from my Aunt Kaitay, she proclaims, "These will do!"

"But . . . but I was going to wear those to the birthday party," I protest. It, of course, is to no avail as Jade defiantly exits my room clutching the conscripted earrings and slamming the door.

It is when I go to my jewelry box to retrieve a substitute pair that I discover my emerald earrings missing. Emeralds are our birthstone, a symbol of the month Jade and I were born. Our father presented each of us with a set of earrings with our birthstone on the day of our twelfth birthday. Mum believes, as did her ancestors, that a birthstone is a talisman of sorts, bringing not only good luck but protection to the wearer. She also says that it has an effect on the wearer's personality and when worn spawns loyalty, courage, and sincerity. She wears a topaz ring given to her by her mother. She claims that is the reason she is always faithful. Ironically, Daddy refuses to wear the ostentatious garnet ring given to him by Mum on their wedding day. I looked up the birthstone for November, the month Mum was born, and found that the topaz signified fidelity and for Daddy the garnet was the birthstone for January, the month he was born, and purports to signify constancy. Daddy claims that that describes his persistence; Mum claims that describes his stubbornness. He, however, says he wished he had been born in December where the birthstone signifies prosperity. Mum says he wouldn't wear the birthstone ring even if it were turquoise. His retort is that he doesn't need to wear a ring to prove his worth.

I am somewhat perplexed at not being able to wear the diamond earrings given to me by my Aunt Kaitay. But I'm more perplexed by the disappearance of the emerald earrings given to me by my father. It was less than a week ago that I wore them at a dinner party hosted by my parents. I'm convinced Jade took them and if I were to search her room, would find them. If I found them, she would claim they were the set given to her, that they were not lost, just misplaced. And if I tell my parents, I am a tattletale. Besides, she would tell them that I was a liar and a trouble maker. They wouldn't know who to believe and we both would be punished. That way, I would be victimized twice for something Jade did. I have learned to accept Jade for what she is and overlook her deficiencies.

Crimson's shrug was only one of many gestures of resignation she had made in the past decade or so and would make in the years to come. Crimson was not usually one to harbor resentment, but she couldn't help but resurrect instances of callous disregard for decency Jade had exemplified in treatment of her siblings. Jade seemed to relish especially in dispensing her brand of deception—a brand that was distinctly and defiantly hers.

Revisiting old hurts was all consuming and had been a preoccupation that had marked and scarred Crimson's early childhood along with having to endure the torment being dealt to her on a constant basis by her twin. The brooding left little room for the happy thoughts that girls her age desired to experience. Through help of a child psychologist, she was able to dwell on the positive rather than the negative. Because of Crimson's loyalty to her sister, which was never reciprocated, Crimson was misdiagnosed. Her anxiety attacks, depression, anti-social behavior, crying episodes and withdrawal from reality were all symptomatic of a mental disorder boarding on psychosis and neurosis, at least according to the mental health experts, all of whom seemed to be in agreement. Never was there an attempt to get to the cause of her acts and omissions. Instead she received heavy doses of medication to contain her mental and functional disorder. Ritalin was her constant companion for the first ten years of her life. Through determination and divine intervention, Crimson's symptoms faded and now at thirteen no longer manifested themselves. Even though disorientation seemed to be one of the symptoms of neurosis, Crimson was able to overcome her disorder through the process of dissociation. By removing from the main stream of consciousness the perceived acts of injustice perpetrated on her by her twin, by her parents and by those in authority, Crimson was able to cope and function in rather remarkable fashion. Her environment would be detrimental only if she allowed it to be so.

As I enter the ballroom at the Fairmont Hotel, I immediately recognize one of my favorite tunes being sung by one of my favorite artists. "Sweet Little Sixteen" was modified to "Sweet Little Thirteen" and was sung as on cue by none other than Chuck Berry. Both Jade and I like rock and roll and Chuck Berry's song "Rock and Roll Music" is right up there with Elvis's "Heartbreak Hotel," "Love me Tender" and "Don't be Cruel." Later we were told by our parents that Daddy haggled over the price with Elvis's manager, Colonel Parker, for the better part of six months and finally gave up booking Jade's favorite artist. They wouldn't divulge the amount Elvis demanded, only that they could have chartered a cruise liner for a hundred fifty guests a lot cheaper. Needless to say, Jade thought it would have been worth the money and will sulk until she tires of it.

I am overwhelmed with all the pomp and pageantry of our thirteenth birthday. "The twins only turn thirteen once," Daddy says repeatedly to Mum. Apparently Mum is not of the same mind as Daddy. She refers to the affair alternately as ostentatious and frivolous as she shakes her head in apparent disgust. With the gifts Jade and I received, we could have opened a small gift shop of our own. Even with a calculator it would be difficult to compute with any degree of accuracy what was spent on the elaborate wrappings, let alone the gifts themselves. I agree with Mum's assessment; Jade predictably sides with Daddy.

As I watch Jade dance with the cute boys, I am somewhat envious. Normally, I am not envious of Jade but my inhibitions and bashfulness relegate me to the sidelines and, though I hate to admit it, Jade is the most popular. I am accused of being standoffish so when Caldwell Harkens asks me to dance, I readily accept in hopes I can improve my image and dispel the notion that I am an introvert.

Caldwell's father is a United States senator and comes from a wealthy banking family. He has been a classmate of Jade's and mine since third grade. He will also be entering the seventh grade this coming school year. He and I have taken several classes together and he aspires to be a forensic psychiatrist. He is a top student and is in the advanced science classes. He helps me in anything scientific; I help him in English literature and composition. If it weren't for his thick glasses with dark rims, he would be the most handsome of all of our male classmates. Jade says he is boring and calls him a nerd. As Caldwell leads me onto the dance floor, Jade spots us and gives me her typical disapproving glance. I ignore her and concentrate on not embarrassing my dancing partner.

Somewhat hesitant and uncertain at first, I soon settle into a comfortable rhythm. Part of the reason is that Caldwell's unorthodox style is attracting a lot of unwanted attention. Mortified, I have no choice but to attempt to divert the attention away from him. My improvisation and abandonment of all inhibitions soon is receiving the acclamation of those surrounding us. I'm sure they all think I am Jade, which would be quite a compliment.

It is while at the punch bowl that I encounter Redondo Courtlin, Jr., whose father is Redondo Courtlin, a famous Hollywood actor who stared in the western "The Last Cross Standing" which, by the way, was nominated for the best picture of the year last year. Redondo is also in our class. It is obvious he is older than the rest of us judging by his maturity and physical stature. He is over six feet tall and has a sleek muscular build. He is dark complexioned and has his father's swagger. He has gleaming white teeth and a broad smile. His eyes sparkle with a zest for life and communicate hopeful exuberance. Just being in his presence is paralyzing.

"You're Crimson, one of the Ziang twins," he says.

"How do you know I'm not Jade?" I ask.

"Just do," he answers.

I can feel my heart race and beat to a cadence rivaled only by the beat of Chuck Berry's drummer. Before I can gather my wits, he asks me to dance. The next thing I know he grabs my hand and pulls me onto the dance floor. I glance at Caldwell and cringe when I see the look on his face as he stands confused and chagrined, balancing an overflowing glass of punch in each hand. I can only imagine what the front of his dress shirt must look like as he hastily sets the glasses down and frantically dabs at the red sticky mess with a cloth napkin. That may account for his mysterious disappearance.

I had been pretty much isolated from Jade and her core of admirers – that is until she spots me dancing with Redondo. When the dance ends, we are surrounded by Jade and her hangers on. With hugs, contrived concern and birthday wishes all around, they greet us. Normally, I am and have consistently been shunned by Jade's friends. It has been as though I had some highly contagious disease. I don't know what Jade has told them about me. I am not paranoid nor am I particularly disturbed by it. I have my own set of friends and much prefer them over those who pacify Jade. For now, I can reciprocate with my own brand of appeasement, although it is not natural for me to be otherwise deceitful or hypocritical.

It is not long before Jade separates Redondo from the pack and I watch as personality exudes from her every pore. It is obvious that Jade is stalking her prey and that the unsuspecting prey is being ensnared in the trap. I'm not dismayed by her blatant actions and feel sorry more for Redondo than I do myself. This has been a typical Jade-like pattern for as long as I can remember. Jade has coveted anything and everything she perceives I have ever wanted or held dear. It is usually not long before the conquered become the vanquished. Jade has a collection of broken hearts. Before long, Redondo will be just another in a long line of her castoffs.

Redondo appears receptive to Jade's charm and before long all eyes are focused on the two as they sway to the rhythmic sounds of Chuck Berry. I dance with one of Jade's friends more out of defiance than desire and watch as Jade performs her magic.

It is at this juncture that the birthday formalities are announced and the ancient ritual mimicked. Jade and I take center stage and endure the platitudes and attention foisted on everyone on this planet whose birthday has been recognized. There are billions of birthdays each year and nothing unique about them. I guess they are special because it is a sign that the honoree has survived another year. Indi says the alternative is not an alluring one. Speaking of Indi, I watch as he and his buddies congregate around the Champagne fountain filling crystal goblets ordinarily meant for the adults. He catches me peering at him and raises his goblet in a birthday salute and mouths "Happy Birthday." I smile and throw him a kiss.

Indi was eighteen in March and will be graduating from high school next month. He is having a difficult time deciding on what college to attend. He seems proficient at everything he does and everything is so effortless. Jade and I have to work hard for our grades and have a difficult time following in Indi's footsteps. It is virtually impossible to live up to the expectation of our parents and the teachers who have had Indi as a student. Both Jade and I would have flunked math this past year if it had not been for Indi. He has been very patient with both of us and, even though he has just cause, never refers to us as his dumb sisters, at least not in our presence.

Indi and I have been particularly close. He has been a great brother. He is careful not to show favoritism and never says anything derogatory about Jade. I marvel at how he controls his anger when he is provoked by her. Being five years older has helped but he has our father's disposition and is never flustered. The tougher the situation, the more calm and deliberate he becomes. I remember when Jade borrowed Indi's tennis racket when she couldn't find hers and in a fit of rage over having lost a match, pulverized it. Even though it was his favorite racket and he hadn't given Jade permission to use it, he never overreacted or told our parents about the incident. Jade never apologized or attempted to replace it. It is much like Jade's helping herself to my jewelry and Mum's. Nothing is sacred in our household, not with Jade on the prowl.

I guess everything is replaceable. However, I recall an incident involving our family pet. Actually, it was a puppy given to Indi by our parents on his eleventh birthday. Jade and I would have been almost six years of age at the time. Indi named the puppy Snowflake. She was a registered bichon frise and the largest and friskiest of a litter of five. She was a cute, loving dog. We all fell in love with her.

When Snowflake was about four or five months old she chewed up a pair of pink cowboy boots belonging to Jade. Even though Jade was told to keep her closet door closed, she never did. Anyway, when my parents refused to replace Jade's pink cowboy boots because of her disobedience, Jade retaliated against Snowflake. At first, Snowflake was nowhere to be found. After several days, Snowflake was found in a plastic bag in the bottom drawer of Jade's dresser. Snowflake, of course, had suffocated. We were all distraught, Indi even more than the rest of us. That was the one and only time I saw Indi cry. It was only years later that Snowflake's replacement appeared on the scene. Tasha is a Siberian Husky that Indi takes with him wherever he goes. He refers to her as his "date." He says that is the only reason he has kept his old Jeep.

Indi and I have had a close relationship for as long as I can remember. Apparently, I had problems with one of my kidneys when I was born and there was concern over whether or not I would lose one of them. According to my urologist, Dr. Timothy

Boran, I was diagnosed with congenital atrophy of the left kidney. Despite its small size, it neverthe-less was determined to be healthy in structure and, according to Dr. Boran, there was no reason to have it removed. When I was in the third grade, I was kicked by a horse at Stormy's Riding Academy out-side Redwood City and my left kidney was damaged. Although no nephrectomy was performed, there is always that possibility and that fear limits some of my physical activities. It was Indi who offered to provide a kidney when my condition was touch and go and who assures me that should the occasion ever arise, he will be there for me.

Redondo was history by mid-summer. Jade and I have not been allowed much by way of serious dating and never outside the company of a responsible adult. I don't know which parent was the strictest. Both were sticklers and both kept pretty good track of the two of us. I never offended but was used by Jade to bend the rules. I guess you would call me an enabler or maybe even an accomplice. Redondo was not the only one Jade would slip away with and I only know what encounters she had as a result of her graphic narratives afterwards. As with most of her accounts, I consider them embellishments and something with which my parents need not be too awfully concerned, even if her accounts are true. Compared to Jade, however, I was and still am pretty naïve.

Seventh grade was ushered in in predictable fashion. Jade won the battle with our parents over the use of cosmetics to some extent. What she left home with and her appearance when she returned from school bore little resemblance to the transformation that occurred the minute she exited the school's girls' room. Several times she was reprimanded by school authorities. Our homeroom teacher, Ms. Thornson, on more than one occasion threatened to call our parents and suspend Jade for the day for violating the dress code. She was able to conform just well enough to prevent that from happening. Mid-year, I was caught in the crossfire when I was called to the principal's office for having been mistaken for Jade. Being the loyal twin that I was, I took the denunciation and chastisement in stride and our parents were none the wiser.

Jade was always trying to cut corners and take the easy way out. Somehow she always escaped unscathed. When I tried to flout the rules, I always got caught. Jade always bragged about being the master of deception and disproving the theory that you can't fool all the people all the time. I'm not sure whether Jade's grand escapes were the product of genius or luck. I suspect a combination of the two. All I know is that she always had bold expectation and the guts of a burglar. I am philosophical when it comes to Jade. My creed, which is inscribed on a plaque that hangs on my bedroom wall, says it all:

Life is too short to wake up in the morning with regrets;
So love the people who treat you right;
Forget about the ones who don't and
Believe that everything happens for a reason.
If you get a chance, take it;
If it changes your life, let it.
Nobody said life would be easy;
They just promised it would be worth it.

I guess I will just have to wait and see if what it proclaims is true.

JADE

IT WAS OBVIOUS WHICH of the Ziang twins, as we have been called, was and is the favorite. I cannot erase from my mind the day when Crimson and I had barely turned three and were in our turquoise and white striped ginghams standing at the front gate of our family home, eagerly awaiting Daddy's arrival. Upon arriving at the gate, Daddy spotted Crimson and after making flattering comments about her outfit, lifted her up and carried her up the stairs leading to the front door, set her down while he opened the door and, holding her by the hand, led her inside. I see myself still standing at the gate watching, heartbroken and forlorn. That has symbolized my treatment ever since and the misery is forever etched in my memory.

One shouldn't marvel at that, considering how we were branded at birth. In order to tell us apart, we were tattooed with the Yin-Yang Chinese symbol which, I have learned, has significance in defining one's future. The configuration is thought to foretell of one's future in this life as well as the next. The white paisley pattern placed first determines a radiant existence, one filled with contentment and rich reward. The black paisley pattern placed first, on the other hand, determines a bleak existence, one filled

with condemnation, mortification and disappointment. Guess which configuration defines my future?
The outcome of my life is preordained and I have
little or no control over it. The Yin-Yang configuration is and, no matter what I do, will continue to be
an albatross around my neck or more aptly my right
ankle. It is predestined that I always be at the wrong
place at the wrong time and living at the whim and
caprice of some undefined external force.

I have been denied a happy childhood by my
heredity and environment. Everyone around me is
judgmental, especially my parents, siblings, teachers
and even my friends. I don't seem to be able to do
anything right—at least according to their assessment. I don't measure up to my parents' expectations and feel their loathing, the scorn of my brother
and sister, the ridicule of my friends and the disdain
of my teachers. There are days I wonder about my
heritage and, if it weren't for the mirror image of
me I see in Crimson, I would think I was an adopted
child. The more I heard the story about Cinderella,
the more I could relate to the stepchild status and
the pain she must have felt being shunned by those
closest to her. Her plight is a painful reminder of
the predicament in which I find myself. When I'm
Indi's age, I will distance myself from the hurt and
pain and, like Cinderella, will turn the tables. No bad
deed deserves to go unpunished. At the top of my list
are my parents. Close behind is Indi and, of course,
Crimson.

Turning thirteen should be a joyous event, at least according to my closest friend, Tonja Morley. Tonja is in the eighth grade and will be fourteen in May. She is allowed to go out on dates unchaperoned and stay out until midnight. Her parents are not controlling like mine and she is pretty much allowed to make her own decisions. She is an only child and, therefore, is not shadowed by a pesky brother or sister. I am not allowed a sleepover at Tonja's unless Crimson is included. Crimson is in cahoots with my parents and is their eyes and ears when they are not around. I've gotten to the point where I don't tell Crimson anything I don't want my parents to know. I don't trust either Crimson or Indi and feel they are trying to widen the gap between my parents and me.

Today I turned thirteen. I will be a teen for the next seven years. I was curious about the definition of teen in the dictionary. The first definition was the traditional one. The second was not. Teen is defined in *Webster's New World Dictionary* as anger, wrath, grief and suffering. When I told Crimson that both definitions fit me, particularly the second, it precipitated an argument. So what else is new! It seems Crimson thrives on controversy and preaches that it is time for me to get off my pity pot. Easy for her to say when she is the favored twin.

I don't really want to go to our birthday party. I already know what the entertainment will be. When we were asked by our parents who they should select to perform, I chose Elvis; Crimson wanted Chuck Berry. Since Crimson always gets her way, it is a forgone conclusion that it won't be Elvis. I argued that Elvis was already becoming scarce and that Chuck Berry would be around for a long time to come. Crimson didn't appear to listen to a word I said. This was somewhat surprising considering that we both were fans of Elvis. It just goes to show the great length that Crimson will go to agitate me. She seems to know what buttons to push and how to make me look bad. Yet, she is the one everyone perceives as wearing the halo.

My patience is tested when I open my closet door and find the dress I plan to wear to the party is wrinkled. Mum had given me a choice and persuaded me to wear my least favorite dress, which had been pressed for the occasion. The hem is much too long and makes me look like a Sunday school teacher. Also, as I try it on, it reminds me of a smock worn by our neighbor's cleaning lady. I absolutely refuse to wear it.

"Mum," I yell. "The dress I plan to wear to the party is wrinkled. Can I get it pressed?"

"Jade," Mum says in typical dictatorial fashion, "we went through this discussion yesterday. Didn't we agree on the white brocade hanging on the door? It is a lovely dress and similar to the one Crimson will be wearing, only in a different color."

"I don't like silk," I say, "especially the gold design which makes it look like the uniforms worn by the waitresses at Chi-Yens."

"Child," Mum says, somewhat irritated, "you picked the material and the design and the dress was custom made to your specifications. It appears you are just being difficult."

"Oh, all right!" I blurt. "I guess I don't have a say in what I wear like Crimson. I'll just wear my raincoat over it just to make everyone happy."

Mum just shakes her head and purses her lips, a signal that she is not in the mood to discuss the matter further. I can't imagine she would keep me from attending my own birthday party if I pursued the issue but I realize it would be to no avail anyway. Mum is stubborn and will not be coaxed into submission. Until I am of age, I must conform to her dictates and the dictates of everyone else.

I reluctantly slip into the replica of Daddy's waitress uniforms. The gold design is oriental in nature and is set off by the white silk background. It looks better on and in the last analysis may not be such a bad choice after all. It was expensive and looks expensive and there is a chance that it won't find a duplicate, other than Crimson's, at our birthday party. There is also the likelihood that it will be imitated by others at future events. Such a dress is one of a kind only once. This may be the one and only time I wear it. It is like leftovers that are thought to have the element of staleness and repetition and are therefore no longer desirable.

My exuberance is dashed as I rifle through my jewelry box looking for my emerald earrings. It is frustrating when Crimson borrows my jewelry and clothes and doesn't return them. She accuses me of doing the same thing without any real proof. Some things are hands off but she doesn't seem to respect her own things, let alone mine.

I will have to admit that I am a little miffed when I enter Crimson's room and pluck my birthstone earrings from her jewelry box. Don't ask me how I can tell the difference between her emerald earrings and mine but I am certain the pair I seized were the same ones Daddy gave me. I also spot the set of diamond earrings which each of us was given by our Aunt Kaitay. As expected, Crimson denies having seen my birthstone earrings and protests as she sees me leave with the diamond earrings. Later, I find the missing emerald earrings in a jacket pocket but decide to keep Crimson's pair in retaliation for her hostile attitude and unwillingness to share. Because of her mental disability, which everyone denies, she'll ultimately either lose them or give them away, anyway. I will actually be doing her a favor, as I did when I used to hide her meds.

I am dismayed as I enter the ballroom at the Fairmont Hotel. Just as I had predicted, my parents booked Chuck Berry. I should have used reverse psychology and, in all probability, Elvis would be the entertainment. With Elvis's limited appearances, it is very unlikely we will ever be able to book him. Daddy paid a lot of lip service in relating his attempts in engaging Elvis as the entertainment for our thirteenth birthday. Apparently, he succumbed once again to the wishes and demands of my sister and had no intention of ever scheduling Elvis. I doubt it was the money, as Daddy has more than he can ever spend.

Crimson accuses me of wallowing in resentment. She chides me for never being satisfied with what I have. As I look around the ballroom I see friends and classmates whose parents have a lot more and give a lot more to their children. It is not just riches they shower on their offspring but, unlike my parents, time and attention. More time and attention are directed to Indi and Crimson than to me. Yet Indi and Crimson also feel deprived. I feel I am tolerated rather than treasured. It is a feeling I am unable to dispel and one that I have had since birth. I don't feel sorry for Crimson and feel she has used her congenital birth defect to garner unwarranted sympathy and attention. She has been told repeatedly by her doctor that there is nothing to suggest that her left kidney will fail. Even if it does, she still has a spare. My feelings are temporarily placed on the back burner as I am surrounded by my friends. The first to greet me and wish me happy birthday is Dorian Decker.

Dorian and I have had a thing for each other since third grade. He is one of the tallest in our age group and his most distinguishing feature is his sandy hair bleached by the constant exposure to the sun's rays. He spends most of the summers on his father's sailboat and the whites of his eyes encircling dark blue irises stand out on his deeply tanned face like chalk on a blackboard. The same thing is true of his pearly teeth. His metallic braces glimmer when a beam of light strikes him. He is not the brightest star in the classroom but when it comes to football, basketball, baseball and track he is just the opposite. He has also been the perennial class president as long as I can remember. His greatest claim to fame, according to him, is me. He is the only one who accepts me for who and what I am.

When Chuck Berry plays the first bars of "You Never Can Tell," Dorian and I find ourselves in each other's arms adrift on the dance floor in a sea of our admiring guests.

"How does it feel to be as old as I am?" he says with a broad smile.

"You'll always be six months older than me!" I say with a twinkle.

"Being a teen is not all that it is cracked up to be, you know," he says somewhat somberly.

"I'm not sure I catch the drift." I lean back and look him squarely in the eyes.

He frowns. "Much more is expected by our parents, teachers, coaches and everyone else. We are no longer able to use the kid crutch to lean on and the adults are not as tolerant. Plus, my parents give me a lot of chores that I hate and that interferes with my sports."

"That's the way I have been treated all my life," I say. "It can't get much worse. Everything seems to get pushed off on me now and I don't expect things will change. Indi and Crimson are treated like royalty while I am treated as an interloper without any rights or privileges of my own."

"You poor thing! Just look at you in that expensive dress and jewelry that all the rich and the famous would kill to have. And, here, let me see the calluses and blisters on your hands." With that, Dorian stops dancing and grabs both of my hands, turns them palms up, and pretends to examine them with the precision of his physician father. He then shakes his head in contrived concern. "We should probably call for an ambulance and have you taken to the ER."

When he asks me to turn around so he can examine the scourge marks on my back, I tell him he is missing the point. "Psychological abuse is much worse than physical abuse. If you could only see my emotional scars, you would be much more sympathetic and understanding."

Before Dorian can respond, I spot Crimson out of the corner of my eye. Dorian spots her about the same time and asks, "Isn't that Caldwell Harkens dancing with Crimson?"

"One and the same," I say, shocked that Crimson would be dancing with the most annoying and repulsive boy in our class. "I just hope no one thinks it is me who is dancing with Caldwell."

"Well, now that I think about it, it is rather difficult to tell the two of you apart—at least looks-wise."

"I assume you refer to my preternatural personality."

"I don't know what preternatural means but if it means unusual, then I agree."

"Do you mean that as a compliment or as an insult?"

"As a compliment, of course!"

I snicker as I watch Crimson and Caldwell dance. Crimson appears unabashed and even bold, despite the spectacle Caldwell is making not only of himself but her as well. I almost feel as though Crimson is doing this out of defiance in an effort to embarrass me. She can't compete with me otherwise and would risk tarnishing her own reputation to ruin mine.

In the middle of the next dance during "Sweet Little Thirteen," Chuck Barry's version of "Sweet Little Sixteen," Dorian whispers in my ear: "She has gone from one extreme to the other. Guess who your sister is dancing with?" I strain to see past the couple next to us. Crimson is now in my sight and I am stunned when I spy Caldwell's replacement. Crimson is dancing with none other than Redondo Courtlin, Jr., a hunk who has never given me even a second glance. "From a nerd to a sophisticate," I say loud enough for Dorian to hear. I can't believe I said that. Apparently, Dorian is of the same mind, as he gives me a wry smile and a look that says he agrees with me.

"After the dance is over, we need to hang with Crimson and Redondo," I say to Dorian. "After all, she is my sister and it is the least I can do since we share the same birthday."

I have a difficult time focusing on the dance, even though it is played in Crimson's and my honor. I direct my glance at Crimson and Redondo every chance I get. I am not very coy and a bit too obvious, I'm afraid. As the dance ends, Dorian asks if I am pre-occupied with my sister or with her dancing partner. It was meant as more of a derogatory comment than a question. I ignore it and grab Dorian's hand and lead him in Crimson's direction. We are soon joined by a cluster of followers. Dorian and I greet Crimson and Redondo with hugs and everyone follows suit with greetings and birthday wishes for Crimson.

I can tell Crimson is skeptical of my motives. With a disapproving glance, she gives me space to greet Redondo. When she engages Dorian in conver-sation, I ask Redondo to dance. He does not appear eager or reluctant. When Redondo looks to Crimson for approval, she hesitates only momentarily before nodding.

Redondo is taller than I expected and easy to dance with. We say little to each other that is unneces-sary as I feel his closeness. Even though we passed each other in the hall and smiled at each other from time to time, we really had no prior contact. Strangely, it is as if we have known each other a lifetime. Neither of us is willing for the dance to end and feel comfortable continuing to dance with each other, especially when we see Crimson and Dorian now dancing together.

When it is time to blow out the candles, cut the birthday cake and open the birthday gifts, Redondo stays close by. Since he positions himself on my side of the gift table, I assume that is a signal that he has abandoned Crimson. His eyes also convey a message that when the music begins again, he and I will start where we left off. And that is exactly what happens. It wasn't me who lured Redondo away from Crimson; it was Redondo who pursued me. I would never do anything to purposefully hurt Crimson even though I would be perfectly justified in doing so.

To make a long story short, Redondo and I ended up going steady for the remainder of the school year. We were inseparable until about mid-July when Crimson and I left with our parents for Europe. In Paris, I met and for several years corresponded with Maurice Vasarely. He was a little over a year older than me and someone Mum and Daddy greatly disapproved of. Maurice made me forget about Redondo. For the next several years, I could only dream of being with Maurice.

For some of the school dances, I found myself paired back with Dorian. Nothing was the same with either Redondo or Dorian after my ten days in Paris. Although Redondo later tried to date Crimson, she was unyielding and determinedly resisted his advances. Crimson told Indi that she was not interested in my rejects. While in Paris,

Crimson had met a budding tennis player by the name of Adrien Jardine. It is obvious she had developed a crush on him and that he has become her favorite preoccupation.

Seventh grade is a drag. I don't feel challenged and feel we are wasting a lot of time on things we will never use. Both Crimson and I are enjoying our exposure to the French language and our study time together. Even though both Maurice and Adrien speak fluent English, Crimson and I aspire to live someday in Paris and, if we are so lucky, it is imperative that we be able to speak fluent French. Being a romance language, we find it particularly alluring. If the children in France can learn to speak French, we are confident we can do so as well.

My favorite classes are English Composition and English Literature. I relish them and look forward to being a novelist as well as a poet. Written expression is intriguing, particularly poetry where the rhythm of the words and their arrangement paint a vivid image. Whoever said "a picture is worth a thousand words" has never read or written poetry. One of my favorite poets is Percy Bysshe Shelley. One of Shelley's poems defines my plight in childhood and now as a teenager and my inability to reverse the curse with which I am inflicted. It reads as follows:

> *We look before and after; we pine for what is not.*
> *Our sincerest laughter with some pain is fraught;*
> *Our sweetest songs are those that tell of saddest thought.*

PART FIVE

IN THE STILLNESS OF DARKNESS

CHENZOI

THE TELL-TALE SIGNS WERE ALL OVER, only we failed to recognize them. First were the uncontrolled outbursts of anger and frustration. Second was the challenge of authority that escalated with the passage of time. Third was the total and unconditional rejection of appeasement. Fourth was the unwarranted condemnation of Lanzu, Indi and me. Fifth was the scorn and distain she showed towards her sister and anyone who opposed her. Sixth was the accumulation of a rather large sum of money she claimed was earmarked for college. Seventh was the mysterious disappearance of cash from various areas of our home, including her father's study. Eighth was her insistence on privacy of calls made to and from her private landline telephone. Ninth was the secret bank account she had established in a Sacramento bank. Tenth was her recent incessant devotion to the Internet and her cloister-like existence just prior to her departure.

We would have made pretty ineffective detectives. All the evidence was there and we failed to heed the warnings. As has been said, the obvious oft goes undetected. At least she had the decency to leave a farewell note. That was June 5, 1976, a Saturday and less than a week after her eighteenth birthday.

I am still shaking as I re-read the note Jade left and I recoil as I think of the absurdity of the reasons for her abrupt and unexpected departure. Even though it has been over five years ago that I first read Jade's farewell, I still feel an indescribable sadness to which only a mother can relate. I fight back the tears as I re-read.

   Dear Mum and Daddy —

When you read this, I will be hundreds of miles away. No, I have not been kidnapped and leave only because I chose to. As you know, I was born with a stigma— one that defines me and my future. But for divine intercession and intervention, I would have been the first born and Crimson would be the one writing this letter.

I never asked that I be treated any better than Crimson, only that I be treated the same. As an infant, child and adolescent, the family's attitude and perception of me never changed. In fact, time has only enhanced the malevolence and disdain you all have for me. It is a curse that can no longer be ignored. To absent myself from your sight is something you have long sought and a wish I'm powerless to resist.

As you have no doubt concluded, my decision is not precipitous. I have thought about it long and hard. In fact, I have agonized over it to such an extent that it has affected my mental well-being and even to some extent my physical well-being as well. I can no longer contend with the rejection and the contempt that has been foisted on me.

I know life is not fair and that it may be possible to follow an alternate course, although it appears impossible at the moment. I must at least make what I hope will be a life-altering decision, one that will be in my best interest since I am the only one who is looking out for me.

If you two feel abandoned, then you know how I have felt the last eighteen years. If I don't leave now, I will have no one else but myself to blame. I am my own person and feel a freedom I've never experienced before. Please be understanding and allow me the space I so desperately need. I'm confident I can make it on my own and it is a foregone conclusion that all of you will be better off without me.

Jade

Just like that, Jade left in the stillness of darkness and neither her father nor I had even a premonition. As I reflect back on Jade's life, I see a soul who looked but didn't recognize; a soul who heard but failed to heed; a soul who spoke but didn't communicate; and, a soul who touched but didn't feel.

To the uninformed, there may be some validity in Jade's assertions. But to those of us who shared Jade's first eighteen years, the assertions are just that and are unfounded and absurd. To set the record straight, our sin was not oversight but overindulgence. Jade and Crimson, if anything, were idolized by their brother, Lanzu and me. The twins were placed on a pedestal. One was not favored over the other and to this day we do not love one any more than we do the other. I have no idea where the opposite notion originated or why it has pervaded Jade's thinking. Just because Jade thinks it doesn't make it true. But, for her, truth is irrelevant and reality is what she considers it to be.

In November, I will be fifty-one, the start of my second half century on this earth. In July, within weeks of Jade's withdrawal from the family, I started having respiratory problems. I had trouble breathing and submitted to a series of tests that determined that I had lung cancer. Obviously, it was not related to smoking since I had never smoked and was seldom around people who did. I am under treatment at the moment and am optimistic about the outcome. Lanzu has been a great comfort to me on all fronts. With all that is happening, I am concerned about Crimson and Indi. Crimson will turn twenty-three in May and Indi turned twenty-eight in March. Crimson is following in the footsteps of her father and me and graduated from the University of San Francisco in 1980. She has delayed her plans to attend law school until the fall of 1982.

Indi received his Bachelor of Science Degree in Business Administration in 1975 and is working for an accounting firm in downtown San Francisco. He is being groomed to take over the family restaurant and currently is doing the accounting work for our family businesses. Neither Indi nor Crimson has married and both still live at home, much to the delight of Lanzu and me. We know it is just a matter of time, however, before either or both venture out on their own.

LANZU

WHEN JADE LEFT HOME, our family was devastated. Family life, of course, is steeped in Chinese tradition and is considered a sacred unit. Jade was an integral part of the family and it is not the same without her. With the disintegration, none of us is as effective as we were before. Fragmentation has placed us all in crisis and the disarray in which we find ourselves is distressing, to say the least. Where it will lead we are uncertain. We do know, however, that Jade's perceived banishment and stubbornness will be a hindrance in persuading her to return even if she should be found.

I read and re-read Jade's letter, trying to make sense out of it. I remember a professor in college once telling our class that entertaining resentment is like drinking poison and hoping for the other person to die. I didn't think much of the statement at the time but the more I analyze Jade's letter the more significance it seems to have. Leaving home is Jade's mode of retaliation for her perceived mistreatment and even if it results in her own self-destruction and ruination, it will be worth it all, at least according to her calculation, if the intended targets suffer even a little bit. An eye for an eye, a tooth for a tooth! One way or another, she intends to exact her pound of flesh.

Even though Chenzoi does not attribute her acute medical condition to Jade's departure, I do. I have witnessed my wife's mood swings and moments of depression since we discovered Jade missing. Chenzoi is riddled with guilt and blames herself for having turned a blind eye to Jade's plight. "Jade was the one in need of treatment," Chenzoi says, "not Crimson. Jade is the cause of our anxiety and may very well have been the cause of Crimson's anxiety as a child," she adds.

I have to admit that Jade was a very difficult child to raise and upon reaching her teens was more intense and challenging than Crimson primarily because of her craftiness. She pulled the wool over my eyes on more than one occasion. Her rhetoric was hypnotic and, even though I knew she was not always telling the truth, I still always believed. It didn't make any difference what it was or who she was talking to. She was most convincing.

Before Jade obtained her learner's permit, she was caught driving Indi's old Jeep. When she was stopped by the police, she was unable to produce a driver's license or learner's permit or any identification. Her dialogue as to a medical emergency involving a trip to the pharmacy, which by coincidence was located only a few blocks away, resulted in her receiving a citation rather than a trip to the stationhouse. The officer allowed her to drive the Jeep the seven blocks back to our home while he followed in the patrol car close behind. We found out later that he even apologized for having stopped her.

The story doesn't stop there. Although she provided the officer with her correct address and date of birth, she identified herself as Crimson Ziang. Providing false information to the police, I later learned, was a more serious offense than driving without a license. So, unbeknownst to her mother or me, Crimson pled guilty to the citation and paid the fine. Unfortunately, it delayed the eligibility date for Crimson to receive her learner's permit. If it weren't for Chenzoi sometime later finding a copy of the citation in Crimson's room, we would have been unaware of the entire incident.

When I look back, I must concede that Jade was indeed the master of deception as she claimed. The extent thereof may never be determined. Only Jade knows for sure. And, it's a safe bet she's not telling. Her ability to persuade despite the lack of logic is the reason I thought she would be the more likely twin to aspire to becoming a lawyer.

At age fifty-four, I consider myself very circumspect. All my children are free spirits. That is what makes them inquisitive, creative, independent and daring. Far be it for me to judge them. They are individuals with their own talents, personalities and peculiarities. Because identical twins have the same

DNA and Jade and Crimson grew up in the same environment, I incorrectly surmised that they would be the same in more than just looks.

Even though Jade and Crimson think and act differently doesn't mean, as far as I am concerned, that one is better than the other or that one is right and the other wrong or that one should be treated differently than the other or that one is loved more than the other. It simply means that their differences must be recognized and respected and, if they are on the wrong course, that they be guided in the right direction. True love sometimes requires tough love and true love always requires unconditional love. The criteria are not what is in the best interest of the parent, but what is in the best interest of the child. When the two interests conflict, as they often do, then those of the child should trump. As between children, one child should not benefit to the detriment of another or vice versa. In any event, all conflicts should be resolved in a fair and equitable fashion.

I have found that the more you give your children, the more they want and expect and the less they appreciate. My quandary is what you do when you reach out and continue to reach out and they turn away and continue to turn away. Chenzoi says that you just continue to reach out. I am inclined to do just the opposite, especially in Jade's case. She has been gone five years now and both Chenzoi and I are frantic with worry because we have heard nothing from Jade and it is as though she has fallen off the face of the earth.

Our faith clearly has been tested and if faith develops perseverance, then certainly we should be listed among the indomitable and unremitting.

INDI

IT IS PAINFUL TO WATCH as our family has been torn apart by the insensibility of Jade in deliberately creating a mystery surrounding her disappearance. It is a martyrdom of sorts. Her self-sacrifice in the form of a self-imposed exile was done in an effort to evoke pity and guilt and to cause, from her perspective, deserved anguish and misery. She manipulated the family by her presence and continues to do so now by her absence.

The stress created by the inescapable anxiety has taken its toll on my parents. The internal turmoil has manifested itself externally and is no doubt the cause of the malady for which my mother is being treated and the panic attacks my father has lately been experiencing. Even Crimson has become somewhat withdrawn and morose. An unremitting gloom has pervaded the Ziang household, so much so that even our closest friends are reluctant to socialize with our family and do so only out of a sense of duty.

Our parents have provided each of us with opulence of which others only dream. When I graduated from high school, for example, I was given a congratulatory card with a set of keys to a white Chevy Corvette. I was also provided with my own credit card, which my parents continue until this day to pay. I have never abused the privilege and, being provided my board and room by my parents, I have few extraneous expenses. What is not covered by my credit card I pay out of my own pocket with the earnings from my employment.

Upon high school graduation each of the twins was presented with keys and the title to a white diamond Cadillac convertible. To my mother, white symbolized spiritual connection and, being particularly superstitious about the color of vehicles in which she rode, ours were always white. The twins, too, were provided with their own credit cards that were billed to my parents. Jade's credit card, however, was cancelled by my father two weeks after her disappearance. When the final bill arrived at our home the following month, it was anticipated her whereabouts would be determined by her credit card purchases. Such was not the case. In Jade-like fashion, she was careful to cover her tracks. In checking the newspaper ads and making the appropriate telephone calls, we discovered that Jade had sold her graduation present to a local automobile dealership. That was a clear sign she had skipped the country.

How long Jade had been squirreling away money and in what amounts we don't know. When the statement for her savings account came, it showed a withdrawal on Friday, January 4, 1976, of $98,414.22. The statement for her checking account revealed that when she closed the account on the same date as the savings account, it had a balance of $12,816.36. If Jade were frugal she could live on those amounts for quite some time. With what she squirreled away and received from the sale of her white Cadillac, there's no telling how long she could survive on her own without requiring a bailout. And, because of her cleverness, there's no telling whether she has left the Bay Area or whether she is still living in our midst. More likely than not, she is living on some remote isle in the Pacific.

Crimson denies she had any advanced notice of Jade's departure or where Jade is currently residing. I believe her, but it would not surprise me that, to respect her sister's confidence, Crimson has not told us everything she knows. Crimson's loyalty towards her sister, though never reciprocated, is legend. She is the glue that is now holding our family together and she must feel terribly conflicted knowing that all of us are fraught with worry awaiting some word as to Jade's location or overall welfare. Crimson is fairly closed mouthed and careful not to speculate, at least not outwardly. She says she doesn't want to create false hope. Perhaps she is frustrated and exhausted, as am I, in trying to second guess Jade. In the past, that has proven to be an exercise in futility and a dead end, not just for her and me but for our parents as well.

CRIMSON

MY MOTHER'S LIFE has been guided by signs of the zodiac and belief that we all come under the influence of certain signs, depending on our date of birth. For example, she was born between October 23 and November 21 and, therefore, under the sign of Scorpio, which is symbolized by the scorpion. Jade and I were born between May 21 and June 20 under the sign of Gemini, which is symbolized by twins.

What is not common knowledge is Jade's dependence upon the zodiac, including the Chinese zodiac. She believes the constellations are the major determiners of one's future along with the elements of air, earth, fire and water. She claims her ruling planet (along with mine) is Mercury. That is curious, inasmuch as Mercury is the smallest of all the planets and the one closest to the sun. In fact, it is so tiny that it is a mere speck and ordinarily cannot be seen except through a telescope. Its ancient symbol resembles the biological symbol for female.

Jade has been able to find a hidden meaning in everything and claims that all things have an astrological connection, no matter how remote or speculative. For example, she considers Mercury as an insignificant planet and, in turn, herself as insignificant and valueless. She is much more talented than any of our friends or relatives, including myself, and yet has a low opinion and almost a loathing of herself. She is tentative, lacks confidence, and is filled with anxieties. However, to those who do not know her well, she appears to be just the opposite.

Even though the Chinese zodiac lists admirable traits under what is called the third animal trine consisting of three animal signs (tiger, horse and dog), Jade prefers to adopt the least desirable traits as those defining her and thus her future. The admirable traits are being dynamic, engaging, enthusiastic, honorable and independent. The least desirable traits are being anxious, disagreeable, hot-headed, moody, quarrelsome, rash, rebellious, reckless and stubborn. Apparently, those born under the three signs are resistant to suggestions.

Jade claims that timing is everything and that everyone's course of conduct is guided on the basis of the time of day or night. I never quite grasped the nature of her system, only that she considers a time period she calls "Xushi," between seven and nine p.m., as the most sacred. This was the period during which she usually did her homework and studied for her exams. It was as a result of Jade that I was introduced to mnemonics, a technique using formulas and acronyms to improve the memory. Like our mother, Jade was superstitious and had a centaur talisman that she wore and would not allow anyone to touch. Laden with shards of deep purple amethyst, it was shaped like a horse but contained a man-like head, torso and arms. Jade never disclosed its origin, only that its power emanated from the constellation Centaurus.

A week before Jade left home I was awakened in the middle of the night by a strange dream, or rather a nightmare. Jade was surrounded by a group of demonic figures. As they were walking towards me, Jade was admonishing them not to harm me. They seemed to obey her. I could hear her tell them that I would be remaining behind to complete some unfinished business and that she needed to talk to me in private. Everyone except Jade vanished. Jade walked towards me with outstretched arms and a welcoming smile. As we walked towards each other and were about to touch, an invisible barrier of some sort separated us. I could see disappointment in Jade's eyes. I watched as she mouthed "I'm sorry." Before I could respond, the other figures reappeared and ushered Jade away. I tried frantically to find an opening in the barrier to follow Jade but to no avail. I watched as Jade waved a tearful goodbye. I could hear muffled sounds and Jade's groan as they disappeared into the netherworld.

My heart raced with anxiety and a longing to be with Jade. I was mesmerized by the realism of the dream and tried to make sense of its connotation. Before I could ponder the significance of it all, the door to my bedroom suddenly swung open and as I sat up in bed, Jade rushed to my side, cradling her tattered but cherished teddy bear, one that she had had as long as I can remember.

"I just had a frightful dream," Jade said as she held tightly onto "TD" and tears filled her eyes. "I dreamt I was taken away from this place and away from you by some evil force. I was whisked away without telling you I loved you. I know I have been less than the sister you deserve." As we held each other tight, she said, "Forgive me for the pain I have caused you and for blaming you for my unhappiness. No matter what becomes of me, I will always hold you deep within my heart. I will make it up to you somehow, someway, someday."

"I had the same dream," I sobbed. "I will always love you, too!"

After Jade left the room and reality started to settle in, I was troubled by what Jade might have meant by her statement. "No matter what comes of me . . . ." To me, that was not a good omen. All Jade could talk about the past several months was reaching legal age, graduating from high school and being with Maurice in Paris. The only thing left unfinished was for Jade to be with Maurice.

I can understand Jade's longing. All I have thought about since meeting Adrien was being with him in Paris. Both Jade and I dreamt of the day we would be with our beaux in Paris. Daddy was fearful that returning to Paris would rekindle the desire in us

to be with the two young men who posed a possible
threat to our virginity and obviously to our continued schooling. Even though Daddy didn't say so, I've
concluded that was the reason we never returned to
Europe and especially France. *C'est la vie!*

Our two years of Spanish and our two years of
French were the glue that held Jade and me together.
Jade had a phenomenal memory and breezed through
the language courses. I did so only with great effort
and my competitive spirit. Both Maurice and Adrien
were fluent in English, which made it easy to communicate. By the middle of our second year in French,
Jade and I were able to read and write well enough
to communicate in French. That way, if any letters to
or from our respective pen pals were intercepted, the
intruder would have no clue as to their meaning. The
same thing was true of letters written back and forth
between Jade and me to Maurice and Adrien. The
French language was our form of encryption and our
most effective way of ensuring privacy with respect
to our romantic communiques.

From time to time, Jade and I would share our
intimate musings and even allow the other to review
the correspondences we received via the French connection. Jade, for the past month or so, seemed to be
more guarded than usual. I suspected something was
amiss the week before graduation when I entered her
room. She thrust what seemed to be a letter under
some other papers on her desktop in an apparent
attempt to keep me from inspecting them. I saw an

empty bank envelope in her wastepaper basket, indicating that some of the documents being camouflaged were bank records. Bank records were not something she ever really shared, but for some time prior to her departure, there had been limits placed on access to her room. Not only did she keep her door closed, she began keeping it locked.

Our birthday was on Sunday, graduation was on Friday, and Saturday was the day we discovered Jade's note and her disappearance. Jade's timing couldn't have been worse. Mum's and Daddy's birthday gift was a two-week trip to the Bahamas, a vacation location selected by Jade. We were scheduled to depart for Miami to stay a few days with some distant relatives on Mum's side of the family the following Monday before flying to Nassau mid-week. Needless to say, the vacation plans were put on hold and, in short order, were scuttled altogether.

Reflecting on the past several weeks and the days leading up to Jade's disappearance, I was troubled by not what I remembered but what I didn't remember. I didn't remember much about graduation and graduation night was particularly a blur. I suspect Jade had put something in my drink. I just remembered wanting to be home. It was after midnight when we left Jessica Wilkers' home in the adjoining block. Fortunately, we did not have far to drive. I remembered being too tired to take off even my dress and crashed on the coverlet. How long I had been asleep I don't know. Half awake, I had the strange sensation

that someone was bending over me. I was too tired
to open my eyes, even when I was kissed on the forehead. I could feel someone put something under my
pillow. The next morning I found my missing birthstone earrings Daddy had given me and the missing
earrings I had received from my Aunt Kaitay that Jade
had taken. Curiously, I also found Jade's talisman.
An eerie gloom envelops me every time I look at it.
However, because it was precious to Jade, it is precious to me.

Even with Jade having left home, I still feel
her presence. She is with me always and I am with
her always. The connection no doubt started at our
moment of conception and is one that persists even
today despite Jade's blatant attempt to dissipate it.
The wedge she is driving between us is one I don't
think she has consciously considered or even of which
she is aware. I have the impression that she would like
to wave the magic wand and make the past just disappear. I can still hear her say, *The past is history and the
future, unless you decipher the signs, a mystery.* Just by saying she's sorry is a step forward but it doesn't erase
all the scars she has caused and the hurts that go with
them.

I have tried to concentrate on the good rather
than dwell on the bad. However, as late as today, Mum
brought up the fact that if I had only turned in my
final assignment in English Composition, I would
have been valedictorian of my high school graduating class. It pains me when I think of it and the role

my twin played in a disappointment needlessly foisted on my parents. I am comfortable having been just an honor student and feel more accepted by my class-mates for not having been a valedictorian. That having been said, I need to explain the role Jade played in all this.

Our final assignment in English Composition was to write a seven to ten-page term paper on the topic "Using Fiction to Inform, Inspire, Convince and Entertain." It constituted twenty-five percent of the final grade. I had written mine well ahead of sched-ule. Jade procrastinated until the last minute and in frustration shredded her draft the evening before it was due. With an F, Jade would receive at most a D in the course. She needed a C or better to graduate. She was very distraught and hysterical to the point that she was gasping for air. My heart leapt for her and to make a long story short, I gave her my paper, which she turned in the following day with her name on it. I, of course, did not turn in a paper. Because it con-stituted 25 percent of the grade, I received a B, the lowest grade I ever received in either grade or high school. To this day, Jade and I are the only ones who know the unvarnished truth.

I have also kept under wraps another secret that could have had a bearing on Jade's chances to gradu-ate. Jade and several of her classmates were involved in a hit-and-run accident during the final week of school. The vehicle they borrowed without permis-sion was Indi's old Jeep. It was uncertain whether the joyride involved the use of alcohol or drugs or both as the Jeep had been reported as stolen and no one was apprehended for the theft. Indi's prized Jeep was totaled and we all consoled Indi in his time of loss. Within weeks, Daddy replaced the Jeep with a 1976 model with all the gadgets. Not too shabby for a second vehicle but still little consolation for Indi having lost Ol' Tinker. The only reason I know Jade was involved was because I helped Jade bandage and camouflage a badly scraped hip. She concealed the pain rather well and no one was ever the wiser.

All my life it seems I have covered for Jade. She has always been frivolous with her life and the mantra she has defiantly articulated as long as I can remember is as follows: *It is my life and I can do with it as I please. No one is affected by my actions but me and me alone.* I'm sure that was her rationalization when she decided to leave home. She has no realization whatsoever of the disaster she has caused and the devastation she has left in the wake of her inopportune departure. It has always been just about her and there is no reason to believe that will ever change.

I feel like I am perpetrating the great deception when it comes to my parents. I feel as though I am a Judas, a Brutus and a Benedict Arnold all rolled up into one. Even though I don't know for certain where Jade is, I have a fairly good idea. Loyalty to Jade prevents me from revealing my suspicions but just as importantly, I am reluctant to speculate for fear it will only create false hope. To watch my parents as their expectations are dashed is not something I could bear and especially not at this time when they are both so vulnerable and Mum so fragile.

Suspecting that Jade was in Paris and that maybe by chance Adrien had seen her, I sent several letters to Adrien posing the question. On the day following Labor Day, I received the following reply, *"Je viens de la voir!"* My heart beat faster. He had seen her! I thought it strange that he gave no details. Stranger still is that he appeared evasive when I wrote back, seeking more information. All that he volunteered was that he had recognized her but that she hadn't appeared to have recognized him.

I wanted to keep the note as proof that Jade was all right, but I was worried that my parents might find it. One afternoon when they were both out of the house, I took it to the backyard and hunkering over a bare bit of dirt in one of the flower beds, burned it. The paper flared, then grew black and finally faded to gray. I dropped the last remnant and ground the ashes into the dirt. Now no one could accuse me of keeping my sister's whereabouts from them.

Prior to the sighting, Adrien had expressed a desire to make his first trip to the United States in mid-October and I had, believe it or not, obtained Mum's and Daddy's permission to allow Adrien to stay at our home. In fact, in the next to the last correspondence I received from Adrien, he had penned next to his signature, *"A l'un de ces jours."* And, his last note, received on Monday, September 20, 1976, asked the question, *"Faut il venir?"* In response, I quickly wrote a note back in French, saying, "You have to come!"

He didn't come and never wrote to me again. Was my behavior too brazen for his taste? Or had he found another girlfriend? I am afraid to write and ask.

Since then, I have reoccurring nightmares of Adrien glaring at me. Looped through his arm is Jade, clinging like a star-struck school girl. The look in Jade's eyes is one of vengeance and sadistic satisfaction; a look that haunts me to this day. The logical conclusion is *Il l'ame!* If he loves Jade instead of me, I guess that is something I will have to live with. My Prince Charming has ridden off on his white horse not with me but with my twin. Or, more aptly, Jade has ridden off with my Prince Charming. As Jade would chide, *That was preordained! Que sera sera.*

JADE

I HAVE PONDERED PREDESTINATION and infinity, as have many others. I have come to the inescapable conclusion that I am not in control of either destiny or time. Although humankind professes to have free agency or free will, it is an aberration. From the beginning of creation, there has been a supernatural compass directing our course of action, a map that each of us instinctively and systematically follows. It is the built-in mechanism called an irresistible impulse that compels us to act or not act in a certain way, even though we find it to be abhorrent and even detrimental to our own well-being. If that weren't true, then every being would always adhere to the right and refrain from the wrong.

I have given up trying to control my emotions. It is a losing battle. What I want to do and what I am programmed to do sometimes are diametrically opposed. Obviously, I will end up doing what I am programmed to do; nothing more and nothing less. It has taken me almost a quarter of a century to figure it out. Just doing what comes naturally is less challenging and thus follows what we call the law of nature, which is designed to ensure the survival of the species or at least survival of the actor. That is our internal compass. That is what makes us what and who we are and what distinguishes us from each other.

Externally, my guiding light from as far back as I can remember is found in the cosmos, or more particularly in the constellations—all 88 of them. The configuration of the stars and grouping of the planets are like looking into a crystal ball. They foretell the future and their positioning, particularly at one's birth, I believe, is definitive of one's destiny. At birth it is like fast-forwarding the film of one's life or reading the last chapter of a novel first so that we know how it is going to end. That way, there is no anxiety or false hope or wasted motion. The shortest distance between two points is a straight line. The direct way avoids the delays, disappointments and dead ends. There is absolutely no way to cheat one's destiny, and the inevitable will win out every time. So, *why would one want to endure futility if one is unable to avoid the inevitable?*

I remember when Daddy was showing us the sights of Paris. We were headed for Versailles because Daddy wanted us to tour the Palace built by King Louis XIV in the seventeenth century. He refused to use a road map or stop and ask for directions. Instead, he relied on his memory and instincts, both of which proved faulty. He ignored the road signs and Mum's navigational skills. With dogged determination, we drove a circuitous route, passing some of the same landmarks several times before reaching our destination. When we finally reached the Palace of Versailles, we could see that the road was being cleared of debris from a twenty-plus car pileup. There were a number of ambulances on the scene and we passed several headed in the opposite direction with their warning sirens and flashing lights activated. Later we learned that there were at least a half dozen fatalities and numerous injuries as a result of the accident. This all apparently occurred in our lane of traffic an hour earlier. We estimated we were delayed approximately one hour by Daddy's stubbornness. I'm the only one who didn't call it a coincidence. *Our survival was pre-ordained.* It was in the stars and scripted since the beginning of time. Daddy was only doing what he was programmed to do, something over which neither he nor any of us had any control.

Daddy has always said that persistence over-comes resistance and that all things are possible. He claims it is only the fool who leaves everything to chance. There are calculated and uncalculated risks and, according to Daddy, you should not take any risks at all. What Daddy fails to realize is that whether you take a risk, calculated or otherwise, or don't take any risk at all, the consequences have already been determined and are totally beyond our control. *It was meant to be!* is more than just a slogan; it is a truism and a fact of life. The key is to know prospectively and not retroactively what was *meant to be*. It is like finding the hidden key in the Bible. B I B L E, of course, is the acronym for Basic Instructions Before Leaving Earth. It is the blueprint or footprint, much like a

fingerprint, that labels us and defines our future. It
foretells of future events and thus our future—much
like the stars.

I think people are placed in our path for a reason. Maurice was placed in my life as a passage to
freedom. But for the excited expectation he created,
I never would have survived high school. Because of
him, I was able to tolerate intolerance, rejection, and
isolation. Where there was hatred, he provided love;
where there was injury, he provided pardon; where
there was doubt, he provided faith; where there was
despair, he provided hope; where there was darkness,
he provided light; and, where there was sadness, he
provided joy.

I so looked forward to being with Maurice
from the moment we met. For six long years, we
had a torrid romance brewing via letters *par avion*.
A long-distance courtship for such a long period of
time bespoke of our commitment to each other. The
plan was long in place before my departure for Paris.
Despite the interference of Daddy, I was determined I
would be with Maurice. After all, it was preordained.
It was predicted in the stars. Soon it would be a *fait
accompli*.

Maurice's birthday is October 25 and he was
born in 1957. He is a Scorpio and as predicted, was
secretive, passionate and intense. However, unlike
the characteristics associated with the Chinese zodiac

sign of the Rooster, he did not prove to be straight-forward, trusting and honest. In fact, he was just the opposite. He, or the stars, perpetrated the great deception. More likely than not, it was my interpretation that was flawed. Maybe there is no such thing as infallibility.

I guess turnabout is fair play. I'm sure my family considered my departure in the middle of the night without even a hint to be deceptive. I had no choice. I thought Maurice didn't, either.

My grand escape from my family bondage took some long-range planning. The bank withdrawals and intricate arrangements were not easy. To go undetected for so many months required great skill and planning. I couldn't have done it without Rachel Jianlei, an old high school classmate. She is the one who picked me up when I sold my graduation present and who hid me before driving me to San Francisco International Airport. She and I have grown close and Rachel plans to visit me in Montrouge, a suburb of Paris where I reside.

On Sunday, June 6, 1976, I departed on Air France on a nonstop flight to Paris. I followed the pattern and the protocol formulated by our travel agent when our family flew to Paris while Crimson and I were still in junior high. I left San Francisco International Airport at approximately three forty-five p.m. and landed at the Charles de Gaulle Airport near the city of Paris at approximately eleven forty a.m. the following day, only thirty minutes past the scheduled arrival time. The estimated airtime, considering Paris time was eight hours ahead of California time, was just a little over ten hours.

The time went by quickly and I was glad I had a window seat. Seated next to me in first class was an attractive, stylish lady in her mid-thirties whose name was Dora Duquesne. She had married a foreign exchange student from France upon their graduation from the University of Southern California. She had been visiting her parents in San Francisco and was familiar with Chinatown and, of course, had eaten at Chi-Yen's on several occasions. It was obvious from her demeanor and appearance that she had either been born or married into a family of means. She spoke little of her husband's family and often about an aunt who had just sold the movie rights to her latest novel. Her name was Judith Blevins. I recognized her name because I had read her first novel, *Double Jeopardy*. Madame Duquesne, upon learning of my interest in writing, provided me with her aunt's address. She also gave me her own telephone number and address after first eliciting my promise to meet her for lunch after I had settled in.

I did not recognize Maurice right away, even though he had been sending me his most recent photographs. I blamed the sunglasses. He was taller than

I anticipated and obviously didn't look at all like the Maurice I had met some six years before. The sunglasses and the pencil-thin mustache were deceptive enough. But his piercing dark eyes, his chiseled manly features and his swagger reminded me of a movie star. I suddenly felt insecure and unworthy. It was obvious he stayed close to the gym. I was drawn to him as never before and melted in his arms as the touch of our lips imparted a forbidden offer and acceptance.

As we waited at the baggage claim and later walked through the airport maze toward the parking area, Maurice appeared nervous and tentative. Since I was somewhat self-conscious myself and apprehensive, I did not think much of it at the time. I thought his anxiety was much like my own. I had lain awake many a night fantasizing about that first time when the two of us would be alone together.

Traffic-wise, it was as if I hadn't left the states. The people looked and acted much like what one would observe in California as people hustled to and from lunch. In some respects, they were even more casual and serene.

Maurice had insisted on taking me into the city to one of his favorite sidewalk cafés on one of the main boulevards. It was Monday and I was surprised, though I probably shouldn't have been, at all the street activity. And, there was nothing quaint about Thiberts. The upscale café was owned by one of Maurice's uncles. Oncle Byno, surprisingly enough, spoke perfect English but reverted to his native tongue

when he was told by Maurice that I spoke French.
From time to time, however, he would revert back
and forth from one language to the other, depending
on the expression on my face. Maurice had apparently
told him that my family owned a famous restaurant in
San Francisco.

Monsieur Marseille, our waiter, who claimed
the next largest city in France had been named after
one of his ancestors on his father's side, was particularly attentive. He apparently had been instructed by
Oncle Byno to give us royal treatment.

"Le petit dejeuner" Maurice told Marseille. With
the eight-hour change of time, it was my breakfast
time. That also made it easy for me to order in French,
"Crepes et un chocolat chaud" I said in perfect French.

"Oui, mademoiselle," he replied. *"Et avec cela?"*

*"Donnez-moi du beurre et de la confiture, s'il vous
plait,"* I answered without hesitating. That was a
canned response for which I can thank my high school
French teacher, Mademoiselle Cormier.

When Monsieur Marseille asked, *"Mademoiselle
desire-t-il quelque chose d'autre?"* Maurice, noticing my
hesitation and puzzled look, intervened. *"Non, c'est
tout!"* he said politely. *"Merci beaucoup, monsieur."*

After I had enjoyed my pancake with butter and
jelly and my cup of hot chocolate, we said *au revoir* to
Oncle Byno and headed for the *appartement* complex
owned by Maurice's father in Montrouge. Maurice
was managing the six-story apartment building and
lived on the first floor in a four-room apartment

consisting of two bedrooms, one of which was used for an office, a dining room with an adjoining kitchenette and a parlor. For now, he said, I would be occupying an apartment with a view on the top floor. When I looked at him inquisitively, he explained his parents were old fashioned and would disapprove of him cohabiting with a woman to whom he was not married. I told him I understood even though I was not totally convinced of the rationale. "Besides," he said noticing my stare, "I have to be located on the ground floor to be available to the tenants and I don't want to subject you to the noise and interruptions. I don't imagine I will be managing the complex too much longer."

Taking one of the elevators to the top floor, Maurice led me to apartment 1658. All the floors had four numbers, with the first number being "1" followed next by the floor number, then the *appartement* number, which consisted of two numbers. My residence had a solid glass front and an unobstructed view of Paris. In the distance I could see the iron framework of the Eiffel Tower. The tower boasted a height of nine hundred eighty-four feet, and on our previous visit Daddy wondered why the builders hadn't added the measly sixteen feet needed to elevate it to an even thousand feet. Forty-two years after it was built, in 1931, the Empire State Building opened its doors, according to Daddy, and was twenty-five percent taller than the Eiffel Tower, even without counting ESB's television tower. So he said and so I bragged to

Maurice. Apparently, only the Sears Tower in Chicago is taller. As Maurice stared at the landmark with me, it was obvious he was as awed at the sight as I was. "Next time we are on the Champ de Mars in Paris, I will take you up in the elevator to our family's favorite restaurant," Maurice promised. True to his word, during the next several months, we dined there on several occasions.

My disappointment was erased when I discovered Maurice had assigned me one of the four corner penthouses. It was furnished with ornate antique furniture the likes of which I had seen only in fashion magazines. Even though our home in San Francisco was considered to be lavishly furnished, it did not compare to my new residence at 1658 Cambrai Appartements, 28 Rue St. Marquis, Montrouge, France. Unité 1658 was uncharacteristically large, with seven coordinated rooms three bedrooms, a dining room, an elaborate kitchen, a spacious parlor and, to my liking, a bathroom with a whirlpool and all the amenities. With the plush carpet, Unité 1658 reminded me of a palace.

On the wraparound *balcon* I could lounge outdoors in my birthday suit unobserved. The pool and the workout area were opposite Maurice's office/living quarters. Maurice had managed to have at my disposal all the exquisite linens and silverware needed to complete the aura of grandeur. One of the *placards* was fitted with a wine rack laden with an assortment of expensive French wines. A bottle of Champagne was prominently encased in ice in a quaint but elegant ice bucket next to a large, solid silver, ornate tray of seventeenth century vintage containing an exotic array of hors d'oeuvres—all represented to be indigenous to the region. The accompanying crystal tray with both recognizable and unrecognizable French pastries was particularly alluring. "A banquet fit for a queen," I said in English.

"Beauty deserves the best," Maurice replied in English and then repeated it in French, *"Beauté meriters le meilleur."*

As delectable and inviting as were the trays, they were not the center of our attention. Once the Champagne was uncorked and the first taste barely savored, I found myself disrobed and holding in my hands a bouquet of lily-white gardenias framed by deep purple, almost black, orchids forming, curiously enough, a design similar to the tattoo on my right ankle. "Copied from the photograph you sent me of you basking in the sun in your bikini beside your San Francisco swimming pool," Maurice said. "The orchid was selected because the ornate expression of the petals reminds me of your sensual lips. The glossy leaves of the gardenia and its fragrance remind me of the way you look and feel and the presence of that inviting scent that is so distinctly yours. The white gardenia, obviously, signifies the purity by which you offer yourself to me this day." He then added, *"Tu es une tres belle femme!"*

I was enraptured by that rhapsodical and whimsical moment in which he called me a beautiful woman and everything in retrospect is surreal. Even now I am enthralled by the events of our first night alone together. It truly was something beyond even my wildest imagination and a memory embedded forever in my mind. That is why I am distraught over the revolting change of events that would alter forever my feelings for Maurice and the beginning of the end of our relationship.

France in general, and Paris and its surrounding area in particular, were quickly becoming my Camelot and Maurice my King Arthur. That is, until that fateful day in July, less than six weeks after my arrival, when I encountered the incomparable Fayette Cannes. I shall never forget that day. It was coincidentally Bastille Day, July 14, the day commemorating one of the important events that occurred during the French Revolution in 1789. Nor, will I forget Fayette.

Standing, holding a newborn child, and involved in a heated discussion with Maurice outside the apartment complex was a tall attractive dark-haired girl I later learned was but seventeen years old. With the looks and figure of a Parisian model, Fayette was brash and animated when I arrived on the scene. It was obvious Fayette intended to use her clenched fist to inflict grievous bodily injury on Maurice at all costs.

It was only when I shouted *"Excusez-moi!"* several times that the argument abated. Maurice was very flushed and seemed at a loss for words. Fayette uttered some profanity in French at both Maurice and me before pushing me aside and, carrying the baby like a loaf of bread, abruptly and determinedly headed for the parking lot.

Ushering me into his office and locking the door, Maurice interspersed his explanation with a mix of French and English, none of which made much sense. When he regained his composure to some extent, he admitted to having had an affair with Fayette and being the father of the child that had been born only days after my arrival in Paris. He said this was the first time he had seen his new-born daughter, as he had deliberately stalled seeing Fayette. Or, at least, that was what he admitted to and what I interpreted from his garbled explanation. Judging from the confrontation I had just witnessed, that appeared plausible.

In tears, Maurice tried to take me in his arms. My reaction was to move away, but I managed to recip-rocate with a half-hearted embrace. It was not long, however, before hurt became anger and anger became rage. I pushed Maurice away rather forcefully, causing him to fall backwards over a small coffee table. He pursued me as I headed for the door. Impulsively, I hit him across the face with an umbrella I retrieved from a stand by the door. Later, when I found I had broken his nose, I experienced, surprisingly enough, little remorse. I felt compromised by Maurice's actions and the predicament in which I had been placed. I was not used to being on the receiving end of deception and didn't like at all how it made me feel.

In the ensuing months no matter how Maurice tried, our relationship faltered and would never be the same. In fact, nothing was the same. Even Maurice recognized his attempts at reconciliation were futile and that I was just going through the motions. He, too, soon became disconnected and I suspected Maurice had made peace with Fayette and had been burning both ends of the candle. Destiny, or more aptly fate was not something either Maurice or I could cheat; it was dictated by the stars. The positioning of the planets made the inevitable unmistakable. If only I had not misinterpreted the signs.

It was the first Saturday of September when I telephoned Dora Duquesne desperate for a sympathetic ear. Having experienced an emotional overload and responding to the advice of a psychoanalyst I had seen for the first time two weeks before, I had moved out of the Cambrai Appartements into the Fontainebleau Appartements. At least when I lived at the Cambrai I had someone to talk to, albeit someone I loathed. Here, I had no one. The tradeoff was peace of mind. Still, with the weekend ahead, I craved companionship. I have never been much of a loner and felt particularly deprived the past several days.

Madame Duquesne seemed eager to visit despite having had a house full of weekend guests. She proposed that we have lunch at one of her favorite restaurants and we agreed she would pick me up at the front portico of the Fontainebleau the following Tuesday. Promptly at eleven-thirty a.m. on that cool fall day, Madame Duquesne arrived in her late-model Mercedes and, as she and I met, we embraced amidst a range of emotions that culminated ultimately into a joyous reunion. She was very cordial and very talkative. In no time, she was brought up to speed on the happenings of the last ninety days and my whirlwind affair with Maurice. She not only validated my decision to sever the relationship but gently scolded me for not having done so sooner. She said that when she hadn't heard from me she had a premonition that I was enmeshed in some type of emotional turmoil.

"It was Bastille Day and Jacques and I were vacationing at our favorite resort near the Mediterranean Sea," Madame Duquesne said. "We had just spread out our towels and were enjoying the sun when a heavy cluster of cumulus clouds started gathering overhead. As Jacques and I watched, I spotted a giant cloud take on the form of a bird or what I would describe as a rooster. Then, in slow motion, it transformed into what appeared to be a great white horse."

As Madame Duquesne looked towards the heavens and traced the path the cloud traveled with her hand, she said, "It stayed intact and did not change form as it passed gracefully across the sky."

"Unusual," I said.

"Not as unusual as what next occurred," she said and, while arching her eyebrows, continued. "I could see your face, not in the clouds but in my mind. It was as vivid then as it is today. I immediately sensed distress and disappointment. When I told Jacques, he convinced me it was my imagination. Wish now I had telephoned you."

"Me too," I replied. "I could have used a soft shoulder to lean on."

"Well, you've got one now," she said as she gave me a warm smile.

My ears had perked when Madame Duquesne said the word "rooster." Maurice was born under the Chinese zodiac sign of the Rooster. The dissipation of the fluffy rooster had symbolic meaning, as did its transformation into the fluffy shape of a horse. The Chinese zodiac is thought to be prophetic and to foretell of compatibility. Crimson and I were born under the sign of the Dog, which is a sign that purportedly is compatible with the Tiger or the Horse. The Chinese zodiac was trying to convey a message that I had previously failed to heed. Perhaps Madame Duquesne's vision of a horse was a window into the future and portended of Maurice's replacement.

As Madame Duquesne drove into the hub of Paris, my eyes caught the reflection of the sun's rays on the diamonds embedded in a gold cross that hung prominently from a gold chain draped around Madame Duquesne's neck. I had noticed it when she greeted me but had not paid particular attention to it since. The more the diamonds glimmered in the sun, the more curious I became.

"Madame Duquesne," I finally said, "I am mesmerized by your diamond-studded cross. Is it a family keepsake?"

"Before I respond," she said, "I beg that you be less formal. After all, I sense we will be best of friends and besides, I am not really that much older than you. Please call me Dora. That is my nickname. My formal name is Dorinda, a name that no one in my family calls me. And, speaking of formality, you seem to have a formality about you that is rather unique and intriguing. I assume that stems from your upbringing."

"I never really thought of myself as being formal," I responded. "My parents are both well-educated and taught us communication skills at a very early age. Both my sister and I shed baby talk about the time we learned to walk. Dinnertime challenged the extent of our vocabulary and Daddy was a stickler when it came to focusing upon the systematic arrangement of words. It was also a time to discuss world events and the important issues of the day. My parents taught us to think and articulate our thoughts at an enlightened level. It has held Indi, Crimson and me in good stead socially and obviously academically. Private schooling and having attended finishing school have also left an indelible impression on me as well as on my brother and sister and are also responsible for the way we think, act and talk. What you hear and see is the product of years of programming and the cloning process."

Dora, as I now called her, smiled broadly and, with her eyes on the road and hands on the steering wheel, said, "Sounds like we had the same parents. I was brought up the same way. I have been accused of being privileged by my birth and surroundings and, as an only child, that is probably truer than even I care to admit. However, the standards at home were set so high that I always considered myself deprived and somewhat of a victim. I envied my playmates and for years resented my parents. It has only been within the last several years that I recognize that whatever successes I enjoy, I owe to my parents and their unrelenting love and devotion."

"I envy you for having reached that point in your life," I said. "Unfortunately, I am unable to be nearly as forgiving." Dora reached over and squeezed my hand, transmitting understanding, commitment, and an acknowledgement of parity. Or, at least, that is the way I interpreted it. She met my nervous laugh with one of her own. I squeezed back my promise of unremitting loyalty and devotion before her hand left mine. The newly established covenant, I prayed, would never be broken.

"I guess I never did answer your question," Dora said as we navigate our way cautiously through the noonday traffic. "This cross is more than a family keepsake. It is my security blanket. I would be lost without it. It was given to me by Aunt Clovis, the sister of the aunt I mentioned when we first met and whose name and address I provided you. It was given to me at the time of my confirmation and I have carried it with me ever since. It was blessed by a cardinal during my visit to the Vatican some years ago. I revere it and someday when I get to know you better and we have more time, I will tell you about its miraculous powers."

"I take it you are Catholic," I said.

"Was," Dora replied. "When I married Jacques, I converted to Judaism. His father was Catholic and his mother was Jewish. He was born and raised Catholic but converted to Judaism upon his father's death several years before we met. I'm really a hybrid and from time to time find myself attending a Catholic service. After all, most of France is Catholic and I was born and raised Catholic, and Jacques has no problem with that."

"Maurice was Catholic," I said. "A poor one at that," I added, trying not to unduly dwell on the recent unpleasant past. "But enough about Maurice and me. I want to learn more about you and your cross."

"How many generations this cross has been in the family is unknown," she said as she touched it reverently with a free hand. "It can be traced back to my father's great-great-grandmother. I am told the cross, which is pure gold, originally did not contain diamonds. They apparently had been inserted at the direction of my grandfather upon the birth of Aunt Clovis, my father's sister. Aunt Clovis was the last of six children and one of only two females. My grandfather, overjoyed with the birth of another daughter, had the diamonds embedded in the cross to serve as a symbol of love, beauty and purity to accentuate the cross which to him and his family represented the crucifixion of Jesus and thereby the nexus between heaven and earth."

"Obviously, the cross is a reminder of the redemption of sins and the price Jesus paid so that our sins would be forgiven," I said. "I know that from my own Christian upbringing."

"The symbolism doesn't stop there," Dora persisted. "According to Aunt Clovis, the cross symbolizes the union of opposites and the merging of the horizontal and vertical planes. If you notice, a cross not only extends in all directions but it also draws from all directions. It is its centrality or merging of opposites, so I've been told, that connotes unity and it is its nucleus that represents the connection between us all."

I was intrigued by what Dora related and thought back to a time when I religiously wore a cross around my neck and the day I removed it, thinking it to be folly and mere superstition. It was actually after I broke up with Maurice that I started wearing one again. That was mainly as a result of the prodding of my psychoanalyst, Dr. Maureen Dupree, a non-practicing

Catholic, who convinced me that wearing the cross would ward off evil and that the cross's four extensions were the divine sign of everlasting life. I then thought of the solid gold cross and chain I had left sitting on the nightstand beside my bed, a reminder of my own desolation.

Even now, I have misgivings about wearing the symbol of peace and tranquility and a lingering doubt as to its power. My faith thus far has resulted only in shattered dreams. And it is not just the cross that has failed me. Even the alignment of the stars and the positioning of the planets have left me in somewhat of a quandary, and as for the prophetic nature of my dreams, they, too, are veiled in obscurity. I no longer hear the whispers of an inner voice and, at the moment, am distressed at being alone and forsaken. The firmament provides absolutely no solace.

Dora noticed that I had suddenly become quiet and pensive and challenged my silence by changing the subject. "Have you eaten at Julien's?" she asked.

"Not that I am aware of," I managed to respond.

"It is a quaint little restaurant located on the Champs Elysées in the famous Argent Pentoufle Hotel," she says.

When we reached the hotel and parked the Mercedes, I had this indescribable feeling that I had been at this place before. Even the concierge looked familiar and acted as though he recognized me.

For lunch, I ordered *poulet roti* which came with a *salade* of mixed greens. Dora seemed solicitous and, as to the unpleasant happenings I related that had occurred since we last saw each other, she was most sympathetic. She gave me the name of a local health club and spa and recommended that I explore shiatsu, a Japanese style of massage utilizing pressure points, as a form of relaxation. She also gave me a booklet on *I Ching*, an ancient recipe for obtaining knowledge and insights by the clever use of hexagrams. I was open to anything that might provide the key to the future and the hidden dimensions of life but was not yet ready to abandon completely astrology or my exploration of the symbolic aspects of dreams.

Though I have become somewhat of a cynic, I have found value in deciphering or at least attempting to decipher the signs that have been placed in my path that are intended to provide the clues of my destiny. Even though I can't cheat my destiny, I can at least get a glimpse or sneak preview of things yet to come. That is why I am open to Dora's alternative methods of divine discovery that may provide a window into eternity.

Before leaving Paris, Dora took me on a tour of some of the sacred sites such as the Basilique du Sacré-Coeur, Notre Dame de Paris and the American Cathedral. In each, she insisted I join her in a short prayer. She seemed intent upon helping me in finding *the* answer. By day's end I had found a sense of solace—something that had eluded me for a long, long time.

On Tuesday, September 21, I receive a call from Dora. It had been two weeks since the two of us dined at Julien's. She is eager to speak to me and announces that she has someone she wants me to meet. She won't divulge his name, only that he might be someone I recognize. Remembering Dora's recollection of a vision of me amidst the cloud transformations back in July and eager to get on with my life and forget what's-his-name, I readily accept.

After I hang up the telephone, I have a flashback of a reoccurring dream I have had nightly the past several weeks. It involves Dora and the concierge who greeted us at the Argent Pentoufle Hotel two weeks before. Why the hotel and the concierge seem familiar to me is puzzling in light of the fact that I don't ever remember hearing of the Argent Pentoufle Hotel, let alone ever being there, and the concierge is someone I would have remembered had we previously met. Nonetheless, both have been the focal point of my dreams, and the image of the concierge in particular seems to be indelibly etched in my mind.

I have been standing outside under the portico of the Fontainebleau Appartements but a short time on that overcast fall evening, Saturday, September 25, when I spot Dora's Mercedes come into view. As the car approaches, I can see Dora on the passenger

side in the front seat and a distinguished looking gentleman, who I presume to be Jacques, her husband,
behind the wheel. I can make out only the silhouette of a male figure positioned behind the driver in
the back seat. Before I can clearly see his face, I have
this vision of a photograph Crimson had shown me
some time back of Adrien posing in his uniform on
the front steps of the Argent Pentoufle Hotel. No
wonder the hotel and the concierge look familiar!
The hotel is the APH and the concierge is Crimson's
beau, Adrien Jardine.

"Oh, my God!" I blurt.

"You look like you've just seen a ghost," Dora
says as she steps out of the Mercedes and greets
me. At about that same time, Adrien emerges from
around the back of the vehicle and gloats upon
observing my reaction as he approaches. Both of us
are at a loss for words. Fortunately, Jacques, by this
time, has exited the Mercedes and, all smiles, introduces himself. With the awkward moment averted,
or at least downgraded, all of us began to speak at
the same time.

"I am pleased that the two of you recognize each
other," Dora says.

"I am glad that we finally meet," Jacques says.

"I didn't think you knew who I was," Adrien says.

Still in shock, I mumble something that vaguely
sounds like "It's really you!" Our handshake turns
into an embrace and Adrien and I just stare at each
other before Dora interrupts. "Well, let's not just

stand here. We have reservations at Palermo's. Hope everyone likes Sicilian."

I am still in a daze as we drive away from the Fontainebleau into the drizzle of Paris. I am still incredulous. I am nodding but not comprehending what Dora and Jacques are saying or even what I am saying in response. I manage to ask Adrien his date of birth. Though surprised at the question, he replies, "January 23, 1955." *I knew it,* I said to myself. *He was born under the sign of the Horse. The Horse is compatible with the Dog and the Dog is compatible with the Horse. And, I wasn't even wearing my cross.*

Adrien is much more handsome than I remembered. Five years and a continent away certainly has blurred my memory. However, it is readily apparent that the nondescript adolescent Crimson and I met in Paris the summer after we turned thirteen has evolved into a fine specimen of male adulthood— devoid of any apparent flaws and pleasant to observe.

Tall, tan and trim is how I would physically describe him. He is handsome in a boyish way and his mannerisms belie his adult status. His deep, dark, penetrating eyes reflect a sensitive, sympathetic and solicitous spirit of a soulful nature rare in the young men with whom I have come into contact, especially recently. There is a certain magnetism or karma that draws me to him. He appears confident but not brash, reserved but not withdrawn, solicitous but not over-bearing, circumspect but not hesitant, and firm but not unreasonable. Since I've gone down this path before, I am reluctant to make any rash decisions or expose myself to further disappointment. Despite what my mind says, my heart says otherwise. And we all know which one usually wins out.

I am jarred back to reality when I realize that Adrien is not for the taking. He is Crimson's beau and heartbreak is not something I can or would foist on her. I would not wish on her what happened to me. That kind of disappointment is something with which Crimson is ill-equipped to deal. Even for me it was overwhelming. For her it would be total devastation and for that reason and that reason alone I suppress my selfish notions about Adrien and vow not to be tempted to violate the trust implicit in my relationship to Crimson and Crimson's relationship with Adrien.

I carefully avoid any meaningful dialogue with Adrien and everything is fairly casual until he inquires as to why I have not let my family know where I am. It is obvious that I have been the subject of discussion between Crimson and Adrien. I now become concerned that he might reveal my whereabouts.

"Few people know that I am in France," I say, "and I hope you will help me keep it that way."

"I assumed that was the case. Despite my relationship with your sister, I will be most careful. You need to know, however, that after I ran into you at the Argent Pentoufle Hotel, I wrote her with the news that I had seen you. I hope I did not let the cat out of the bag. I assure you, I will say nothing further."

"I think the secret is safe with Crimson. Nonetheless, if you have the opportunity, tell her you were mistaken. That way, I don't have to worry about being discovered. Daddy has connections and I don't think it would be long before he would be on my trail. I came here originally to be with Maurice and sever my previous ties. I'm not ready to see or talk to anyone from back home and especially not my family." Noticing the look of disappointment on Adrien's face, I hastily add, "Maurice and I are no longer together. He proved to be a real cad."

Adrien looks relieved and, after a brief moment, says, "I'm not sure I will be in communication with Crimson in the future. After our chance meeting, I put everything on hold, anticipating that I would see you again. I know this sounds crazy, but I haven't been able to get you out of my mind."

My heart flutters. What do I do now? What can I do? None of this is my doing. It is obvious that it was predestined that Maurice and I break up and that Adrien and I meet this way. What were the odds? After all, Dora saw the sign in the sky. And what about my reoccurring dreams? I have been bombarded by what some might consider coincidences all my life. In reality, there is a reasonable explanation for all of this. The message being conveyed is an obvious one and one that cannot be ignored. Adrien and I were meant for each other.

"Hey, you two act as though you have known each other for a lifetime instead of having just been introduced," Dora shouts from the front seat.

"If only you knew!" I reply. "If only you knew!"

"What? You knew each other in another life?"

"Better than that! I knew that Adrien looked familiar when he greeted us at the hotel as we arrived for lunch. He apparently recognized me but I didn't recognize him, at least not at that time. When Crimson and I were in Paris, we met and briefly dated two Parisians, Maurice and Adrien. Adrien and Crimson have been communicating back and forth for five years or so, as had Maurice and I."

"What a coincidence!" Jacques says in disbelief. "Something like this happens only in the movies or in novels. What are the chances that Jade would travel to France on the date she did? What are the chances that it would be at the same time and place, same airlines and same destination as Dora's?" And, directing his comments at me, says, "What are the chances the seating assignment would align the two of you side by side? What are the chances the two of you would have lunch together in Paris and especially at Julien's, a restaurant hidden in the Argent Pentoufle Hotel, in the middle of downtown Paris? What are the chances that Adrien would be working at the same hotel at the same time the two of you would go there for lunch? Dora tells me that that was the one and only time you had been to Julien's. And, what are the odds that Dora would match-make the concierge with the recently available sister of the concierge's pen pal?"

"I don't believe in coincidences," Dora interjects.

"Nor do I," I say. "Embedded in the heavens are

stars whose arrangement provides the key to our future. Nothing is left to chance. Everything is pre-ordained. The signs are visible. All we have to do is recognize and interpret them."

"I will agree that there are hidden messages in everything that surrounds us," Dora says, "and that the power that created all has left nothing to chance. However, I disagree that everything has been prede-termined. True, the Creator knows the results before they occur. But, since we are not robots, we have con-trol over our own actions and change directions of our own volition and not as a result of having been pre-programmed to do so. In other words, the mes-sages we receive are, for the most part, informational in nature and suggestive, although some may be in the form of commands. We, nonetheless, have the free will or free agency to follow them in whole or in part or reject them in whole or in part. We are not forced by He who created us to do or refrain from doing anything except maybe under the laws of nature. And, even then, we have freedom of choice."

"Do you think prophesy or ancient predictions are a way to prepare us for future events or calami-ties or do you think they foretell the future and are further proof of predestination?" I ask.

"I'm not sure I get the drift," Dora says.

"If predicted disasters and cataclysmic events could have been averted, steps would have been taken to do so, don't you think? Otherwise, unfulfilled prophesy would undermine its legitimacy and thus its reliability. Doesn't the fact that the unchangeable, for whatever reason can't or won't be changed, suggests predetermination in some form?"

"If you're asking if some things can't be changed, then I agree with you," Dora says in a conciliatory tone. "However," she continues, "mankind, for the most part, is in control of its own destiny. The fact that scripture predicts that nations will rise against nations and brother against brother doesn't mean that it can't be averted, only that it won't be averted. That is a choice mankind makes. Whatever the choice, mankind will either live or die by it. Whether some supervening force will reverse what appears to be inevitable for the end times is something I am not equipped even to ponder, let alone render an opinion upon."

"It's getting pretty deep in here," Jacques says looking in the rearview mirror at Adrien.

"You all lost me when you started discussing coincidences," Adrien says.

We all laugh. Lately, my belief system has been in flux. There was a time when even if I erroneously thought I was right, I was never in doubt. Now, I'm not certain about anything! Little did I know, that all of that was about to change and that my confidence was about to return.

My life for the most part has been filled with contradictions. Consider, for example, the only two loves of my life, Maurice and Adrien. One turned out to be an ill-advised choice and a nightmare, the other a sagacious choice and a dream come true.

I've concluded that I was blinded as to the message hidden in the alignment of the stars and my own distorted perception of reality in not seeing Maurice for what he really was. I am disappointed in myself. I am consoled because of my core belief in predestination. If it weren't for Maurice, I wouldn't have made my pilgrimage to Paris and thus Adrien would never have entered my life.

After our dinner at Palermo's in Paris back in September of 1976, and having experienced a most memorable and enchanting evening with Adrien, I did some research and soul searching in an effort to avoid the emotional disaster I had just encountered with Maurice. I already knew, of course, that Adrien was born under the Chinese zodiac sign of the Horse. The bad news is that those born under that sign are adept at seduction, are exceedingly impatient and are known as being drifters. The good news is that those born under that sign are energetic and self-reliant and enjoy love and intimacy. Resorting to Adrien's astrological forecast, I found that he was an Aquarius, which defines him as being curious, outgoing and independent. When I compared the benefits with the detriments, I found the benefits far outweighed the detriments. And the detriments, I must confess, I found to be fairly benign.

For the five years of our marriage, Adrien has proven to be anything but prosaic. As I watch Adrien open his Christmas gifts, I have the same fascination, or more aptly *twitterpation*, that I felt five years ago today when the gift I unwrapped was an engagement ring. I am as enthralled by Adrien today as I was then and do not cease to be flattered by his display of unrelenting love and affection.

We started dating the night after we had dinner with the Duquesnes in Paris and have been inseparable ever since. We were engaged on December 25, 1976, and married at a private wedding ceremony at Notre Dame de Paris Cathedral on Valentine's Day, Monday, February 14, 1977. Dora was my maid of honor; Jacques was Adrien's best man. The pastor of Notre Dame de Paris and Adrien's confessor was Pere Christophe De Salles, an elderly priest who looked every bit the part. Adrien's parents, Julien and Lorraine Jardine, and his sister, Vivienne, were the only guests present. Our reception was held at the Duquesnes' *maison* in Paris and our honeymoon was at their chateau in Bordeaux.

My in-laws speak very little English and fortunately I've become proficient in French. Thus, we are able to communicate with each other at an acceptable level. Adrien and I alternate our discussions between French and English. Adrien likes to speak English because he is eager to be well-versed in English and I like to speak French so I can be well-versed in the language of my host country. I maintain my United States citizenship in anticipation of someday inheriting property situated in the U.S. I miss my country of birth but not enough to live there permanently. With extended family in France and having dual citizenship, I now consider France my home. With my circle of intimates being located here and my interests being what they are, I have no desire to pull up my stakes here and live elsewhere.

Adrien and I reside in the same apartment building here in Montrouge where I had lived prior to our marriage. However, we have moved into a larger unit, with the type of view that I had when I occupied the corner *appartement* on the top floor of the Cambrai. It has a spare bedroom that we hope someday will be a nursery. So far, there are no little Jardines running around. With Vivienne being divorced and having no children and Adrien and I having been married now for five years, there is no little pressure on us to produce grandchildren for Julien and Lorraine.

Adrien is a computer programmer for a large medical clinic on the Montrouge side of Paris. It is as a result of Adrien that I, too, have been hired by Rose Medical Centre. I have graduated from being a receptionist and in charge of making appointments to preparing and updating patient files. Record keeping is the highest paid of the clerical positions and I have learned a lot about computers from Adrien. I am at the point in my career where I not only read, write and converse in French but think in French. My memory is what has held me in good stead during my school years and now is the catalytic agent responsible for my advancements at RMC.

I've become very focused on the tasks at hand and in what I consider to be a fascinating career. I have been encouraged by the nurses and doctors in the clinic to consider formal medical training. I've been encouraged by Adrien and his parents to do so as well. I have been commissioned by the medical staff at RMC to accompany them at various seminars and take notes of the lectures and transcribe them for future use. I am intrigued by the subject matter and, in particular, the area of urology, mainly because of Crimson's congenital kidney condition. In discussing my medical interests with one of the clinic's urological specialists, Dr. Bella Medoi, whose father is a medical doctor in Hong Kong, I learned that researchers in China have found the human body's energy center to be the kidneys. They have labeled that energy as chi, the twenty-second letter of the Greek alphabet. Chi is also part of the name of our restaurant in Chinatown.

I have also been invited to observe surgical procedures, which I again find most fascinating. I don't think it is a coincidence that I have been exposed to medicine and the mystifying knowledge I have acquired in the short time I have been at RMC. Even when I view certain x-rays, graphs and reports for the first time, I have this feeling of familiarity that lends itself to medical interpretation and evaluation that is later mimicked by the experts.

On Monday of this week, I spoke with Dr. Sigmund Stein about one of his female patients who had a suspicious spot that appeared on a mammogram and, on a follow-up x-ray of the breast, appeared to have miraculously vanished. When I questioned him further, I determined that the first x-ray, which had revealed the spot, was a frontal view of the breast whereas the second x-ray, which revealed no spot, was a lateral view. I then asked him if it was possible that the x-ray from the frontal view revealed a spot beyond the breast that was actually in the lung. He immediately had me schedule another x-ray of the patient with instructions to focus mainly on the underlying area. To make a long story short, the patient is now undergoing cancer treatment on the left lobe, the portion of the lung immediately behind the breast erroneously thought to have contained the tumor.

A misdiagnosis can be fatal. A patient literally places his or her life in the physician's hands. If a carpenter doesn't cut enough off of the board he is working on, he can always shave off the excess. It is not quite as easy if he makes the board too short. With a physician, particularly a surgeon, the slip of his or her scalpel can cost a patient his or her life. To treat a patient for the wrong malady may also have the same fatal consequences. And, in the case of Mrs. X, delaying the treatment of the lung cancer because of the missed diagnosis could have caused Mrs. X her life.

Up to this point in my life, I have pretty much dealt with the theoretical or hypothetical. There was not a lot riding on my analyses and conclusions. Here, at RMC, there really is no wiggle room or margin for error. Close enough is never good enough! Because things are real, I find myself concentrating not on what is best for me, but what is best for others. I apparently am going through an attitude adjustment and find myself being benevolent. This is due in part to Adrien's influence and might also be something that is the product of maturity.

I have paid little attention to the mystical significance of numbers and only recently have been predisposed to viewing numbers as signs meant to provide direction. I was first introduced to numerology by Dr. Dupree, who provided me with a book that listed the associated meaning of numbers, including those that were found in combination. It was actually Adrien who, while helping me sort my personal effects, came upon *Calculating Your Future by the Use of Numbers,* the book I had earlier received from Dr. Dupree. She is the one who is responsible for piquing my interest in numerology.

"Do you realize," Adrien asks, "that you were interviewed for the receptionist position at RMC on June 7, 1977, and that your first day on the job was Tuesday, the 7th day of July, the 7th month of 1977?"

"Yes, but . . ." I reply, not completely grasping the significance although I was taken aback somewhat upon realizing that I started at RMC on 7-7 of '77.

"That was no coincidence," Adrien says authoritatively.

"I never really gave it much thought," I say. Down deep, I know there are no coincidences and that everything was meant to be.

"Aren't you curious as to what the number seven signifies?"

"Why don't you tell me?" I raise my eyebrows in a provocative gesture half in jest and half irritated because I don't know the answer.

"Well, according to *Calculating Your Future by the Use of Numbers,* seven symbolizes wisdom and careful reflection."

"Here, let me see that."

"Don't you trust me?" he asks as he places the book in front of me and points emphatically at the passage.

"It also says seven is a symbol of sacred vows," I point out. "Were you holding out on me on purpose in an attempt to negate your marital vow to love, honor, cherish and obey me?"

"Not on your life!" he says in French. *"Pas sur votre vie!"*

We both laugh. That is something I've done a lot of since being with Adrien. He is easy going and slow to anger. His calmness even in stress is something I have grown to admire and appreciate. His patience is something I've learned to emulate. He has been good for me!

Adrien excuses himself and leaves the room. Within a short time, he returns with an old family Bible. "I am going to see how many times and under what circumstances the number seven is used," he says.

"Wasn't 777 the mark of the beast?" I ask.

"That was 666," he says with a chuckle.

"Don't think so," I say.

"How much do you want to wager?"

"Looser becomes the other's minion for a week."

"You're on," Adrien says as he searches the Concordance for a cite. Within less than a minute, he quotes from Revelation. "His number is 666."

"So my math is off one," I say.

"No, it's off 111," he chides. "Better get used to calling me Master."

"I guess I will have a whole week to remember," I tease.

We then search the Bible for the references to the number seven. Not surprising, we find close to two dozen such references. Adrien is quick to point out the two scriptures that stand for the proposition that he should not have to do chores at home on his days off work. The first was from Exodus, which stated that work on the seventh day was prohibited. The second was from Hebrews which stated ". . . and on the seventh day God rested."

"Do you know what that means?" Adrien asks mockingly.

"Yes," I say. "It means keeping God's commands or mine, and God's wrath is nothing compared to mine."

"You have made your point," Adrien says in his most conciliatory tone.

"There's another number that keeps popping up," I say.

"Let me see if I can guess," Adrien says as he scans the numbers in the book given to me by Dr. Dupree. "Ah!" he says. "It is number two!"

"Number two?" I ask. "Why in the world did you say number two?"

"Number two represents the struggle between the dark side of life and the bright side. The two energies that are at odds with each other are referred to as the yin and the yang. The yin is the dark side and the yang, according to this, is the bright side. To co-exist in a symbiotic relationship and thus balance the two requires selflessness and placing the needs of others ahead of your own. Number twenty-two, which you mentioned moments ago, symbolizes mastery of one's chosen career."

Hearing my sobs, Adrien looks up startled and confused. He holds me in his arms and asks what is wrong. I just elevate my right ankle and point to the tattoo that was placed there shortly after my birth. "This is a tattoo of the yin-yang symbol," I say between sobs. "With the dark pattern being placed first I have been doomed to a bleak existence. That is something that is and will always be."

"That is absurd," Adrien says trying to sooth me. "I love your tattoo!"

"You don't understand," I say still sobbing. "The symbol yin-yang represents the interaction of good and evil in the world. The outer circle actually represents the universe. The black and white forms within the circle represent the two forces that are at odds with each other. The yin, the dark form, denotes confusion and turmoil. The yang, the white form, denotes peace and serenity. As you can see, on my tattoo the dark form appears first. On Crimson's tattoo the light form appears first. The placement of the forms foretells of one's destiny and is determinative of one's pattern of living. The yin-yang, therefore, is not only the source of life but of death as well. It dictates parenthood and hence the reason I am . . . barren."

I am unable to control my anguish and a rivulet of tears again dominates. I am fortified by Adrien's caress and apparent understanding. If it weren't for Adrien and his unremitting love, I would be unable to function. My inability to produce an heir for Adrien no doubt accounts for much of my anxiety. Revisiting disappointment, I've begun to realize, is counterproductive and is an interference over which I *do* have control.

"The number I had in mind," I finally manage to say, "is nine."

"Why didn't you tell me?" Adrien says trying to distract me away from an otherwise touchy subject. Conferring with his new-found authority, he looks up the number nine.

"Nine," he says, "denotes humanitarianism and the devotion of one's life in promoting the welfare of others." He then looks at me quizzically, no doubt wondering why I had picked the number nine.

"I have to be at work at nine a.m. My office extension number is nine and I am in suite nine. I work for nine doctors and oversee nine clerical stations. The address of the clinic has a number that starts with nine and ends with nine. The same is true of the clinic's telephone number. I was informed of a pay raise on Wednesday, the ninth of this month. Need I go on?"

"I forgot to mention that nine is also a symbol of completion and accomplishment," he says. "No wonder you got a pay raise. Also, I forgot to mention that the number nine represents perfection." Adrien then gives me a look and gesture that signify he sees that perfection in me.

"Notice I don't flaunt it," I say.

"But you have every right to," he responds.

After Adrien leaves the room, I pick up the book he has been reading curious as to what he had written in the margin as we spoke. In the margin next to the number 33, he had written "Jade—please note!" The associated meaning read "All things are possible; nothing is impossible." I vow I will be on the lookout for number 33, even though I know I am unable to reverse the curse.

Before falling off to sleep, I attempt the math and try to make sense of the hidden meaning in numbers. It is perplexing at first and then enlightenment consumes me. *Why hadn't I recognized it before?* I had ulterior motives in seeking employment at RMC and could see only sevens. Now I am dedicated to helping the sick and suffering and for the first time see nines. I have evolved in my concentration and have substituted

selflessness for selfishness. Don't ask me how that
squares with me having requisitioned Crimson's beau
and not even feeling a twinge of remorse.

PART SIX

ON
BORROWED
TIME

CHENZOI

WHEN I AWAKENED THIS MORNING, I opened the curtains just far enough to watch as the sun was peeking over the horizon and casting its rays across the California inland in an effort to reach the Pacific Ocean. The shadows it cast on the opposite wall of our bedroom simulated a face. Not just any face, but the silhouette of what appeared to be that of Jade. The similarity was uncanny. I was able to awaken Lanzu barely in time to witness the occurrence. As we held our breaths and each other close, the likeness vanished almost as quickly as it appeared.

"Can you believe that?" I whispered in Lanzu's ear as he still stared at the spot where the image had appeared.

"No!" He shook his head.

I felt him tremble and attempted to console him in his anguish. I felt terrible I had interrupted his otherwise peaceful sleep with an unhappy reminder of an event that had occurred some thirty years before, an event that had changed our lives forever.

As Lanzu collapsed on the bed, his face buried in his pillow, I experienced the same indescribable sensation that I experienced for the first time in 1976 and many times since following Jade's disappearance.

I lay with Lanzu long enough to hear his deep breaths of slumber, a coping mechanism we both have learned to master.

Washing away some of the dismay, frustration and lost hope, I had occasion to stare at the old, disheveled and pitiful face staring back at me in the mirror. I saw a resemblance of both my father and mother. I also recognized a resemblance of my maternal grandmother. It provided me with some comic relief but not enough to cause me to smile. I always remembered my grandmother as being old and wrinkled.

The face staring back at me in the mirror was that of a seventy-six-year-old who had survived the onslaught of lung cancer and the hardships of thirty years of fret and worry. To those mothers who lost children whom I harshly judged and thought should get on with their lives, I apologize. And especially to those who don't know whether their missing children are alive or dead, I now know their anguish. I have learned to pray not only for my lost child but theirs as well. There is nothing greater than a mother's love for her child—regardless of whether that love is reciprocated.

My visions of Jade both consciously and subconsciously have not diminished over the years and, if anything, are more pronounced than ever. I see Jade wherever I look and even when I close my eyes I see Jade. Whether it is at church, the mall, in a movie theatre, or on the street, I see Jade in the crowd. It obviously has become an obsession. Recently, I watched as a young woman was trying on an evening gown at Macy's department store. Even with her face turned in the opposite direction, the long dark hair and tan skin reminded me of Jade so much so that I thought for a moment that it might be her. My tap on the young lady's shoulder startled her. I was most embarrassed and tried to mitigate my mistake. Her smile conveyed understanding and forgiveness. I guess a mother never gives up looking for her lost child, even if it appears futile.

As I walked away, I recalled the biblical account of the shepherd who had a hundred sheep and left the ninety-nine unattended to search for the one that was lost and, when he found the one that was lost, rejoiced and danced with glee with his friends and neighbors. I hope Lanzu and I live long enough to experience such a moment.

The years have been harsh on Lanzu. I have noticed deterioration in his mind and body just since we celebrated our golden wedding anniversary six years ago. He will be eighty in January of this coming year and has vowed to surpass his mother and father, who died in their mid-nineties. He says he wants to be alive the day Jade returns. I'm not sure that will happen and I watch as his hope dwindles every time he answers the door and opens the mail. His mantra is *No news is good news!* I'm beginning to feel his expectation is unrealistic and that neither of us will live to see

Jade again. I have that premonition and the premonition that, even though I am three years younger than Lanzu, I will predecease him.

I had a dream the night of my seventy-sixth birthday that it would be my last and I watched as Lanzu, Indi and Crimson stood beside my bed with sorrow etched on their faces. The digital calendar on my bed stand read Sunday, February 18, 2007. This is most likely, since that date coincides with the Chinese New Year and is also the month and day my maternal grandmother, after whom I was named, died. My grandmother helped raise me and I always felt a connection even after her death. I hear her whispers in times of crisis and am guided by the signals she sends. My dreams have proven to be prophetic and the latest, I am convinced, is designed to prepare me for the inevitable. It is a revelation that I am reluctant to share even with those I trust most.

I have no expectations about seeing Jade again in this lifetime and there is nothing I can point to instinctively to guide me in that direction. I am perplexed by the inability to communicate either consciously or subconsciously with Jade. Whether flawed or not, intuitively I am convinced that no harm has befallen her. I am also convinced that the stars will point her in the right direction and that her internal compass will keep her on course. In the end, I know all will be well.

LANZU

THE NEXT KNOCK AT THE DOOR we know for certain is going to be her. The next telephone call we anticipate will be from her. And the next card or letter we receive in the mail will be news from or about her. These have been our expectations from the day Jade moved away but unfortunately never became a reality. My great-grandfather always said, "He who waits in eager anticipation for that which is not meant to be is a fool!" He also said, "He who dupes himself has only a fool to blame!" He claims both to be old Chinese proverbs. Whether proverbs or his own musings, both apply to Chenzoi and me and the predicament in which we are enmeshed.

I found Chenzoi staring at her reflection in the mirror earlier today. Her scowl worried me. I noticed no sparkle in her eyes or her usual affable countenance. Instead, I saw a look of mortification, condemnation, disgust and disdain. Upon seeing my reflection, her face flushed in embarrassment and she immediately closed her eyes and turned away. In the past, when she blushed, it was sensual and appealing. This, however, was hideous and uninviting. When I reached out, she did not resist. Entwined in each other's arms, thirty years of grief, frustration and resignation gushed from our eyes—enough tears to float the Queen Mary. That which was never meant to be we now realize will never be.

Chenzoi for the past thirty years has claimed to be living on borrowed time. Chenzoi may not have been the only one who has cheated destiny. In retrospect, I may also have been living on borrowed time. Because of Chenzoi, I had not given up on my desire to live and had endured some troubling health issues of my own. Currently, I classify myself as being placid and languid. My problems have been more psychological than physiological. I don't like what has happened to our family and am discouraged by my own inability to adapt to the current circumstances. Acceptance has never been my long suit and accepting defeat is not in my genes. However, as head of the Ziang household, I take full responsibility for not being able to keep the family together. I don't know whether I was too tough or not tough enough. I suspect the former to be the case. Regardless of the cause, the effect is a most undesirable and untenable one.

Throughout most of my life, I have been referred to as the proverbial optimist. That was in the genes! Facing adversity has always been a challenge and I have the reputation, as had my father and his father before him, of being a shrewd businessman and being able to rise to any occasion. Everything was always half full. Nothing was ever half empty. Sadly, my perceptions have dissipated over time and I find myself second-guessing everything. I now lack self-confidence but keep it a closely guarded secret. Losing self-confidence has also resulted in me losing a goodly amount of my own self-respect. Yet I have to keep up the façade because it is expected of me and because imbued in me is the desire to succeed.

Chenzoi and I have spent many hours discussing what we will do *when* Jade returns, not *if* she returns. That has been our mindset until possibly recently. Time is running out and it indeed appears we are living on borrowed time. However, it is the anticipation that keeps our hopes alive and the driving force that sustains both Chenzoi and me. It is too early to give up. At least, that is what I keep telling Chenzoi in an effort not only to reassure her but myself as well.

With Indi and Crimson involved in what has become our favorite parlor game, *What We Will Do When Jade Returns,* we find renewed hope and contentment in our fanciful speculation, something that lifts us from the utter depths of despair. Perhaps the most elaborate postulation comes from Indi. He suggests, on the basis of our expectations, that we book Union Square in downtown San Francisco, closing off both Geary and Post Streets, and have the mayor declare the day Jade Ziang Day. The public would have an open invitation and the food would be catered, of course, by none other than Chi-Yen's. I forget the name of the group that he suggests would be providing the entertainment but it sounded contemporary and expensive.

Crimson got into the act by suggesting that the festivities be launched by a parade down Post Street. Just thinking about such an event brings a smile to my face and a warm feeling inside.

"It could happen!" I say aloud thinking that the transmission of the sound would make it so. "If you're listening, Lord, make our dream come true! Jade needs us and we need Jade!"

When last we played our parlor game, I detected chagrin in the facial expressions and body language of both Indi and Crimson. Later in our privacy, I mentioned my observations to Chenzoi. With a querulous glance and an air of impatience, she responded by the following rhetorical question. "Haven't you read in the Bible the story about the prodigal son?" That was her only response and quite frankly that was all that was needed to illuminate the light bulb. *How insensitive of me, I began thinking.* I can't fault Indi and Crimson for thinking what I would be thinking if I were in their situation.

It was all starting to add up. We were lamenting the departure of the one who abandoned the family and defected to an unknown location without care and concern for the family. If she returned, we would be placing her on a pedestal and eulogizing her for her insensitivity, desertion, and self-centeredness.

On the other hand, Indi and Crimson have stayed behind to care for Chenzoi and me through thick and thin and have attempted to compensate for the loss of Jade. The two have been the good and faithful offspring, yet they have been relegated to the status of mere servants. Instead of running after Jade and embracing her, bringing her the best robe and putting a ring on her finger, killing the fatted calf and playing music and dancing, we should be embracing and celebrating with Indi and Crimson. Aren't two in the hand worth more than one in the bush? How could we have been so blind? I guess the real question is how can we continue to be so blind and squander away the here and now while gambling on the future?

I'm not sure that is what Chenzoi had in mind by her prodigal son metaphor but if it was, it makes perfect sense.

INDI

"I THINK IT IS THE JIANLEI GIRL again calling asking for you," my mother says as she hands the telephone to me.

"Hello," I say.

"This is Rachel Jianlei-Josselyn," she says in her usual flirtatious fashion. "I was just calling to see if you have heard anything from Jade. I had a birthday card I wanted to send."

"Her birthday was back in May," I say.

"It has been sitting on my desk for several months and I was just wondering if maybe you had heard something. I hope you don't mind me bothering you."

"No bother," I say. "I was hoping you would have heard from her by now, inasmuch as the two of you were such close friends."

"Why no," she replies. "If she had, I wouldn't be troubling you."

"Was that Jade's old friend, Rachel Jianlei?" my mother asks after I hang up. "What is she doing calling you?"

"To begin with," I reply, "her name is now Rachel Jianlei-Josselyn and she's no longer a girl. She's forty-eight, Jade's and Crimson's age, and even though she's married, she still has a crush on me."

"I'm not so sure she is calling because she has a thing with you. I think she is calling to get a status report so she can keep tabs on our family. You know I've never trusted that girl and wouldn't put it past her that she's Jade's eyes and ears."

"I've grown somewhat suspicious myself," I confess. "She does pump me for information concerning yours and Pop's health and she is inquisitive as to how the family businesses are doing and whether Chi-Yen's and the other investments have been turned over to me yet."

"Didn't she ask the last time the two of you talked whether your father and I had a formal will and whether Jade was named in the will? Remember me telling you that that seemed odd?"

"Yes, as to all three questions," I say. "Although she purports to be attempting to locate Jade, she is more intent on learning whether Jade is still named in your and Pop's wills. She has not been at all bashful in asking all the pertinent questions."

"I still have not changed my mind about that girl. I have been suspicious ever since Mrs. Vargas telephoned, informing us about a young lady matching Rachel's description coming into the bank several days after Jade's disappearance, seeking information about some of Jade's bonds. Not too many people knew of Jade's disappearance at that point in time. Your father has always contended that Rachel is the key in locating Jade and I think he is probably right."

"I wonder if there is some way we can trick Rachel into disclosing Jade's whereabouts," I offer. "I could pretend to be interested in her romantically and revive the old high school crush in an effort to win her confidence."

"I have never met the husband that you say she has, but deceit is not something your father would condone, let alone encourage. Maybe you could obtain the information in more subtle and less devious ways. Perhaps the direct approach is the best."

After my conversation with my mother, I decided to take the high road and at least attempt to meet with Rachel. I made my mother promise she would not reveal the nature of my mission to either Pop or Crimson.

I retrieved Rachel's call-back number and telephoned her. There was some hesitation at first but then Rachel agreed to meet me at Chi-Yen's for lunch the following day. At eleven forty-five a.m. sharp, I was informed by one of our hostesses that a middle-aged woman had arrived for what the guest termed a luncheon appointment with Indi Ziang. I immediately told Zhou to seat the lady in the most elegant of our private dining rooms, one that had previously been set up for the two of us.

When I entered the dining room, I was totally unprepared for what I encountered. The specimen of radiance and splendor that stood and greeted me was not that of the giddy teen-aged co-ed that I had reluctantly danced with at my sisters' eighteenth birthday celebration some thirty years before but that of an elegant, sophisticated and dazzling specimen existing only in dreams. I don't know how long I stood there transfixed but it seemed like an eternity and the vision was not something of which a man would ever tire.

If Rachel hadn't extended both hands and broken the silence, I would probably still be standing there in grateful observation.

"Well," she said, "aren't we good enough friends to at least shake hands?"

The handshake turned into a caress and I remembered impulsively kissing her on the cheek. Both of us seemed reluctant to let loose of each other and I can still remember the pleasurable feeling I experienced as I held her near.

After we were seated opposite each other, I observed nature's careful selection of desirable traits borrowed from two races and diverse cultures. Rachel's features, though delicate, were strong and striking. The silky rich black hair and natural skin tone bespoke of her oriental ancestry as did her deep penetrating sapphire eyes. Her teeth were snow white and perfectly aligned either by birth or trips to the orthodontist. Her rosy cheeks and facial tone were no doubt inherited from the European side of the family. Regardless of whether

Rachel was the product of inheritance, environment, cultivation or a combination of the three, she bore no flaws, or at least none that were readily detectable.

"I hear that your family has expanded its business ventures into manufacturing and that you spend much of your time in Shanghai and Beijing," she says out of the blue.

"How do you know that?" I ask trying not to appear defensive.

"I read the newspapers and I am friends with Jin Wei, the son of your old Chinese language professor at USF, who lunches with Crimson on occasion."

"Old Professor Jin," I say somewhat sarcastically. "I forgot he had a son who went to school with you and the twins. I suppose Crimson keeps him current on all our family news."

"You should be proud of Crimson. She has been making her mark in the legal community and it is only a matter of time before she runs for the state legislature or some other public office."

"You remember, before she was hired by Cantaberry, Brussels, Hanover & Greenberg, that she had worked for the District Attorney's office? The family thought someday she would run for District Attorney. She has always believed in the strict enforcement of the criminal statutes and is always trying to turn the windmills right side up."

"Jade has always been my close friend, but I never warmed up to Crimson. Jade constantly referred to

Crimson as Miss Goody Two Shoes."

We both laugh. Although Crimson and Jade are identical twins, the similarities stop there. Crimson was a stickler for adherence to the rules. Jade, on the other hand, liked to skate on the cutting edge and take the calculated chances.

"Speaking of Jade," I say, since Rachel opened the door, "where do you suppose she ran off to?" I try to appear as nonchalant as possible and watch Rachel's expression change from direct to evasive.

"Your guess is as good as mine," she says, avoiding eye contact.

"Come on," I blurt, "you can't tell me you and Jade have not had any contact in the past thirty years?" I hadn't planned on being so blunt, but I remembered my mother saying to be direct.

Rachel starts to bristle. Just then lunch is served. *Saved by the bell,* I muse and cringe. I hope my impetuosity has not led to my undoing. I hope I haven't squandered the first real opportunity to locate Jade. Both of us sit in stony silence waiting for the awkward moment to pass. I know Rachel knows where Jade is hiding and I know Rachel knows I know.

Our head waiter comes in to see if we are enjoying our meal and whether we have enough hot tea. Dai is particularly solicitous of Rachel and that eases the situation somewhat. Finally, I manage to say, "I apologize for the outburst. Our family is frantic with worry and I watch what effect Jade's absence has had on my parents' aging process. Forgive me for my brashness.

My question was not meant as an accusation."

As my eyes are impaled by Rachel's, she softens and I see compassion, understanding and indecision. I can sense she wants to tell me but is conflicted by her lifetime friendship with Jade.

Before Rachel can respond, I reach both of my hands across the table as a symbol of peace or, more aptly, a token of surrender and anxiously await her acceptance of the proffered armistice. It is immediately reciprocated and the subject tabled, at least for the time being.

I am genuinely intrigued by Rachel and have no trouble placing my quest to locate Jade on the back burner. I am already feeling guilty about my original reasons for asking Rachel to lunch. I have been guarded about revealing too much about our family affairs and the health of my parents. Rachel's third degree appears intense and I am still suspicious of her motives. If she is to carry news to Jade for honorable purposes, then I have no quarrel with that. If Jade has ulterior motives and is using Rachel as a pawn to make sure she receives her perceived fair share upon the death of my parents, then I refuse to be an accomplice.

As we wait for our dessert and a fresh pot of hot Chinese tea, I ask about Rachel's parents and her life after high school.

"My parents are now retired, alternating their residences between San Francisco and Las Vegas. My mother enjoys the social life and the shows. My father thrives on the gaming tables on the Strip. My younger sister, Rita, lives in Palm Springs with her husband and three children. My older sister, Jill-Lynn, who was in your class, is married and she and her husband and their two sons live in Ontario, California, where they own and operate a thriving sporting goods store."

"When did your father retire from his medical practice?" I ask.

"He had vowed to retire at the end of the century. Actually, he performed his last surgery in December of 1999," she responds somberly. It is obvious she is close to her father and unwilling to accept the implications of his change in status and reputed health condition.

Remembering her father had received cancer treatment at Loma Linda University Medical Center and that his health might be a touchy subject, I changed the direction of our conversation. "I learned from Crimson that you graduated from Stanford and lived and taught school in Palo Alto for several years," I say. Didn't you go back to school and receive your master's degree from the University of San Diego?"

"You have kept pretty good track of me, as I have of you," she says with renewed interest. "I received my master's degree in 1986. Golly, that was twenty years ago. I still teach math at Harben Junior High and will until I am forced to retire."

"I knew you were divorced and remarried. How's that going?"

"I was married eight years the first time, then single for many years. I married Miles just before Daddy retired. That would have been in June of 1999.

"I think you told me that your husband is an orthopedic surgeon?"

"Correct. I should have had better sense. Having grown up with a father who was a surgeon, you think I would have known better. His career obviously comes first and I know what it feels like to be a widow."

"You never had children of your own, correct?"

Rachel swallows hard. "Not because I didn't want them, because I couldn't. Miles has a son sandwiched between two daughters, all of whom are grown, married and have children of their own. I consider them the same as my own."

Rachel gives me a long inquisitive stare.

"Why are you looking at me like that?" I ask.

"You are in your fifties," she begins. How is it that a dreamboat like you never married?" She tilts her head waiting for my response.

"Don't embarrass me," I say sheepishly. "I never found the right lady. Or maybe I should say the right lady never found me."

"You know I've always had a crush on you, don't you?" she asks in a sexy, tormenting voice.

I don't know how to respond. Such an acknowledgement by the Rachel who attended school with my sisters would have generated little reaction. But

such a statement coming from the resplendent crea-
ture now in my midst engulfs my whole being. I'm
too stunned to even pinch myself to see whether or
not I am dreaming. It is as if I have been frozen in time
and space. Everything is surreal.

"Now it's my turn to apologize," Rachel says as
I try to avoid her gaze. "It was not *my* intention to
embarrass you. How indelicate of me!"

I am enraptured by the moment and seem to
have lost all inhibitions. I am powerless to turn away
and find myself totally and hopelessly immersed in
the sapphire eyes fixed on me, which appear as majes-
tic, vast and alluring as a sea of bright stars in the sky
on a clear night.

Before parting, it was agreed we would meet at
the same time and place the following week. Rachel's
kiss goodbye imparted an unmistakable and tantaliz-
ing promise I was determined would be fulfilled.

As focused as I was in ascertaining Jade's whereabouts and pursuing my business commitments, I
spent the intervening nights fantasizing about Rachel.
Although I had lady friends of some renown and some
of which I was most fond, none was as pleasurable as
I anticipated Rachel would be.

In the ensuing weeks we lunched, cavorted and
commiserated together. For good cause, I found
Rachel to be attractive, seductive and irresistible.
Before long, our friendship evolved into something
much more. It was after the first night of intimacy
that Rachel admitted to her complicity in Jade's

disappearance. After eliciting my sacred vow not to reveal Jade's whereabouts, she told me all. There was relief in knowing that Jade was alive and well and enjoying the good life. There was frustration, however, in not being able to convey to and thus share the good news with my parents and, of course, Crimson. Promises were meant to be kept. Rachel kept hers and now I was compelled to keep mine.

As Christmas approached, Rachel relented at my insistence. In exchange for me providing family photographs, the current Christmas newsletter as well as copies of past holiday mailings, and some business newspaper clippings—all to be forwarded by Rachel to Jade—she would implore Jade to send a letter, note or card to our family so as to put all our minds at ease. She agreed that was the honorable thing to do and a gesture that would be compatible with the spirit of the holidays.

When next we met, Rachel said that it took some doing to convince Jade to compose a letter or note that would be enclosed in a Christmas card that would be addressed to the family. Jade had made it clear, however, that there would be no return address or any indication that would compromise Jade's location. The card would be placed in an envelope addressed to Rachel. Upon removal, it would be deposited in the United States mail. Considering Jade's obscurity for the past thirty years, the scheme thus hatched, in my mind, was progress.

On December 24, 2006, Pop assembled all of us in the living room. He and Mom often did that when they had a special gift they wanted us to open on Christmas Eve, one that could not wait until Christmas Day. His hands were shaking as he held an exposed Christmas card close to his chest. I could see the face of the card and between Pop's fingers could make out what appeared to be the Blessed Virgin Mary holding the Baby Jesus. I will never forget then what transpired.

Trembling as never before and unabashed about his usually closely guarded emotions, he held up a Christmas card for all to see. As he stooped to retrieve the carefully folded insert that had fallen from the card, he wept uncontrollably. With all of us assisting in his consolation, he managed to murmur, "It's from Jade. She's alive." It was pandemonium for the next hour or so. My moral compromising brought joy of unimaginable proportions and not just to my family.

Neither Crimson nor my parents could harness their emotions long enough to read Jade's note aloud. So the task was delegated to me. First I read from the card. It was dated December 17, 2006. It was addressed to Mum, Daddy, Crimson and Indi. It contained the following handwritten message: *Have a blessed Christmas and joyous 2007.* It was signed *Your loving daughter/sister, Jade.* In my heart and for the sake of Crimson and my parents, I hoped she meant it.

It was not until I read Jade's Christmas note that I became emotional. I saw a side of Jade that I didn't know existed. The message seemed genuine and heartfelt.

Dear Mum, Daddy, Crimson and Indi:

The years have dimmed the perceived rejection and resentment I have been harboring within me but not the memory of what I have come to recognize as my loving and caring parents, and my devoted and loyal sister and brother. Though I have not measured up to your expectations or maybe not even my own, I beg for your forgiveness and indulgence in allowing me to blaze my own trail. I have come a long way and have even a longer way to go.

The misery I have caused you is undeserved. However, it has taken me thirty years to realize that. I am still in the learning and healing process. Do not give up on me. As soon as I find myself, I will allow you to find me. I am married but have no children of my own. I have failed you in the latter respect. I hope I have dissipated your concerns by contacting you in this fashion. I think of the days we were together and have conditioned myself to focus only on the good times. Continue to hold me in your prayers and I will do likewise.

Love, Jade

I was moved by what Jade said but more by what she hadn't said but inferred. She has come a longer way than she realizes. Hopefully, self-realization and self-respect are but a stone's throw away.

Mom and Pop held onto Jade's Christmas card and note as it they were holding on to Jade or some lifeline. I guess the card and note are a part of her and the only tangible evidence of Jade's continued existence. Holding onto each other evinces togetherness, something all of us have grown to cherish. The card and note now complete the circle of intimacy and not only are a link to the past, but a link to the present and more importantly a link to Jade and Jade to us.

"I knew it," Mom kept saying, "I knew she was all right."

"But now we know for certain," Pop says as he manages his day's first smile.

"Why are you gloating at me like that?" Crimson whispered in my ear. "You look like the cat that swallowed the canary."

"I'm not gloating," I say. "I'm smirking."

"Why are you smirking then?" she asks feigning agitation.

"Someday I will tell you. Until then you can obsess."

"Funny," she says loud enough to draw the attention of our parents.

I have the urge to share my secret with Crimson but discretion is the better part of valor, or at least so I have always been told. *Our guardian angel is Rachel Jianlei-Josselyn, an accomplice of Jade's and a married woman with whom I'm having an affair,* I wanted to say but thought the better of it.

"What are the two of you up to now?" Mom grumbles as she glares in our direction. "Do the two of you know something you are not telling us?"

"Not me," Crimson says.

"Don't look at me," I say.

I didn't consider my answer to be a complete lie.

It is obvious Pop is still in a state of shock as he heads for his bedroom, taking with him Jade's card and note. "Leave those here!" Mom barks. Pop promptly obeys and heads for the bedroom. It is but a short time before he emerges wearing a broad smile and shaking his head.

"I still can't believe it happened," he mutters as he retrieves the card and note from Mom.

"You better pray this is merely the appetizer," she tells Dad.

"Be satisfied for the moment woman," he yells. "Now I can die in peace."

"You'll probably outlive all of us," Mom chides.

"I hope so," he responds.

The rest of Christmas is just as topsy-turvy.

Two days before New Year's Eve, Rachel and I celebrate our own new year, commencing with an elaborate dinner and cocktails at the Mark Hopkins Hotel followed later by sampling the hotel's guest accommodations.

"What was it you called Jade's card and note?" she asks.

"A good beginning," I reply, hoping the remark would not be construed as being snide. She frowns as she glares at me with probing eyes.

Pulling her close and kissing her gently on the cheek next to her ear, I whisper, "In my eyes, you are an angel and also in God's eyes you are an angel for the joy you provided to all of us this holiday season and I'm not talking just about tonight. You brought hope to the doubting and increased the life expectancy of my parents by at least another decade or two.

"Are you saying thank you?" she asks in her usual saucy way.

"Did you have something else in mind?" I ask knowing she doesn't need much coaxing.

We heralded in the New Year in our own time and in our own way. Both of us are grateful for the events that had unfolded during the last few months of the year and both of us look forward with excited expectancy to a new year filled with infinite promise and more intrigue.

CRIMSON

IT IS NEW YEAR'S EVE AND, though everyone anxiously awaits that magical moment when 2006 is transformed into 2007, no one appears eager to expedite the process and everyone seems content to savor the flavor of the family's new-found hope. Our holiday decorations, I must admit, have been fairly meager over the past thirty years but, as I look around, I am astounded by the dazzling display of this year's holiday trappings. "What a difference a card and a note make," I say, but not loud enough to be heard. Everything this evening has more sparkle, crispness and intrigue than I remember from even before Jade left. There is an aura of splendor, inspiration and anticipation—a sign that fractured hearts are mending. The glimmer of the Christmas tree lights and the shimmer of the endless strands of silver and gold garland entwined throughout our home convey an atmosphere no longer of despair and broken dreams but of triumph and jubilation.

"Hey," the male voice says behind me, "don't I deserve some type of acknowledgment or at least a contrived greeting?"

The voice belongs to Mark, the man whose engagement ring I am wearing and have been wearing for almost two decades.

"Mark," I say, as he kisses me gently on the cheek. "I thought you couldn't make it until later."

"Finished the brief," he says. "Still needs some tweaking but is close to being camera ready."

"I'm proud of you," I say as I give him a real kiss. "Happy New Year, darling. I love you."

"Love you, too," he says as he dabs at his lips.

"Don't worry," I say, "my lipstick is smear-proof."

"In that case, give me another one."

I do and tell him there's more where that one came from.

I grab Mark's hand and lead him in the direction of Mum and Daddy. Although Mum has liked Mark from the start, Daddy is not quite so sure. Daddy for a long time didn't think there was a man alive who was good enough to marry his daughter. Daddy now admits that Mark would be a good catch.

Mark is the grandson of Grayson Cantaberry, one of the original partners in the law firm of Cantaberry, Brussels, Hanover and Greenberg where I am now a senior partner and have been for a number of years. Mark's grandfather is deceased. However, Mark's father, Edward, is still a member of the firm, as is Mark. Nepotism has not been an impediment to Mark's and my marriage. In fact, it has been encouraged by the firm's partners as well as his parents. The delay is as a result of my family circumstances and was the condition upon which I premised my acceptance of Mark's proposal. Mark has been most understanding and has the patience of Job. He has never pressed and I have no pressure to marry except perhaps to provide grandchildren for our respective parents.

"Great party," Mark says as he and Daddy shake hands and he and Mum embrace.

"You know Senator Grant Keanan," Daddy says as he introduces an old friend of the family to Mark.

"Of course," Mark acknowledges as he and Senator Keanan shake hands. "Senator Keanan went to law school with my father's brother, Charles, and I don't know if he remembers me but he moved for my admission to the United States Supreme Court back in 1985."

"I hear you are now working with your father and, of course, with this beautiful woman beside you. In my day, female attorneys didn't look like her," Senator Keanan declares as he chews on the unlit cigar and winks at me.

I give Senator Keanan a hug, avoiding contact with what is left of the stogie dangling from his mouth and say, "How come there were no handsome law school students at USF like you when I was enrolled there?"

"I wonder the same thing," Senator Keanan replies. "It's obvious God wanted to spread the human attributes among his creatures and not make too many lawyers both talented and appealing."

"I'm not sure how to take that," Mark says as I join in the laughter.

Mark is not Hollywood-handsome like Adrien, judging from Adrien's old photographs, but handsome in his own way. He turned fifty-eight in

November and is approximately four and a half years older than me. He is over six feet tall, has a runner's build, is clean shaven and has hair turning gray at the temples. His soft baby-blue eyes dominate his face and belie a shrewd, calculating and determined individual, attributes that have held him in good stead on both the tennis and basketball courts and continues to hold him in good stead in a court of law. He is most considerate and solicitous and is, without question, my best friend and confidant.

As we make our way to the bar maintained by two of Chi-Yen's bartenders, Mark murmurs, "It's ironic that Senator Keanan never recognizes me. I have to remind him who I am each time we meet. I first helped campaign for him when I was still in college. My father was his state campaign chair at the time. I'll never forget me accepting his offer to come work for him in Washington when I graduated from law school. When I applied, he denied having made such an offer and claimed he had no openings. All this was done by way of a form letter signed by one of his aides. I have since concluded that he probably made the same offer to keep all the young naïve worker bees on the hook."

"What, you didn't assert the doctrine of promissory estoppel?" I tease. "He made a promise, you relied on it, performed valuable services, and he reneged."

"You make it sound simple. Too bad I hadn't studied that chapter in my contracts class when I was at

USF. Besides, it was my word against his. All I know is that I felt like a fool in being so gullible."

"What makes him so different than all the other politicians? Aren't they all like that? Does any politician keep campaign promises?"

"You mean government can't operate if it lowers taxes and increases benefits?"

"Only if it borrows money from the Chinese," I say snidely. "You want to borrow a couple trillion?"

"I'll take whatever you offer," Mark says, arching his eyebrows. "Why can't I ensnare you like Keanan ensnared me?"

"Much too smart," I say. "By the way, speaking of smart, did your Uncle Charlie flunk out of law school? You never did say why he hadn't finished."

"Although it is an old family secret," Mark says, "somehow he got crossways with the family and my grandfather cut off the purse strings. My guess is that his partying landed him in jail. No doubt it was for one of his DUIs. However, that is not something my father discusses and not something my grandfather ever discussed."

"Sounds as though your grandfather was a harsh disciplinarian."

"Grandfather Cantaberry was a stickler when it came to upholding the family name. He took pride in it and to tarnish it would have been a capital offense. Whatever Uncle Charlie did was an unforgivable sin and only after Grandfather's death was Uncle Charlie invited to family functions and even then only sparingly. Even today, Uncle Charlie is considered the black sheep in the family."

"Didn't you also have an aunt that no one ever talked about?"

"That was my Aunt Audrey, my father's oldest sister. Don't let on that I ever told you. I've only overheard bits and pieces but apparently she became pregnant when she was a senior in high school. She was sent away to have the baby. She never did finish high school and was never reintegrated back into the family. I've never met my aunt Audrey or, to my knowledge, ever seen any photographs of her. It is my understanding that Grandfather erased all evidence that she ever existed. It is still not a topic that is discussed among the Cantaberrys."

"You must walk on pins and needles," I say to Mark. "I know everyone in the firm is afraid of your father."

"I've always walked a tightrope. When my playmates were pulling stunts or about to, I distanced myself for fear of being implicated. Even the mere accusation would have netted me dungeon time and eventual banishment. I've been covering my tracks my whole life. I've conformed out of love for my mother and fear of my father."

"I know I don't want to find myself on your father's bad side," I say and tense at even the thought.

That Mark is unyielding and seldom rattled are qualities that draw me to him. Although he lives away

from his parents, he is still under their watchful eye
and influence. Their manipulation does trouble me.
Even though Mark is now in his fifties, he is still
Edward's prodigy and Agnes's little boy. Even after he
leaves here tonight he will be stopping by his parents'
home to ring in the New Year. That is tradition and
something he dare not break.

The family room has been rearranged to provide a fairly large dancing area. The baby grand
piano has been moved into the corner at the far end
of the room, and our neighbors, Vera and Conrad
Middleton, retired professional entertainers, are
playing the oldies and smoothies from the '50s and
'60s. They alternate turns at the keyboard and sing
mostly duets. Occasionally, one sings a solo. They are
in the midst of *Moonglow* as we enter the room and
stake out our own quiet corner. We shout "One more
time!" as the music ends abruptly. Mark and I have
adopted our own comfortable style of dancing and
prefer the slower rhythms. We could survive on the
two-step, the four-step, and the jitterbug. To dance
without holding at least one hand we don't consider
dancing. We like the closeness and our bodies touch-
ing. We are also stingy on the gyrations as we strive
for obscurity.

When we've had our fill of dancing and solitude,
we hunt for our drinks but find that they have already
been confiscated. So we head for the bar for fresh

ones. I offer to fetch the drinks as Mark talks with the Bradleys. When I return with the replacements, I find Mark surveying the guests.

"I thought you were through with your reconnaissance missions when you retired from the military. Are you looking for someone in particular?"

He is adept at recognizing my jealous side by what he says is the tone of my voice and the contemptuous look in my eyes.

"I was just ogling the young and provocative of the female of the species," he says to goad me.

I give him a disapproving glance and ask, "Are there any handsome bachelors accompanying the females?"

Mark ignores my sarcasm. "Actually, I was looking for your brother, my tennis nemesis. I don't see him anywhere."

"Indi is helping our patrons at Chi-Yen's to ring in the New Year," I reply. "He is expected to make at least a cameo appearance here tonight before or slightly after the witching hour. He promised my parents he would be home in time to say goodbye to 2006 and hello to 2007 and his obligatory hellos and goodbyes to our guests."

"With his itinerary, don't count on it. He might be saving the hallowed moment for that new special someone in his life."

I squint at Mark. "What are you talking about?"

He just grins. "Don't act like you don't know."

"You think I'm playing coy?" I ask.

Mark recognizes my agitation and, in a hushed tone, blurts, "Rachel."

A thousand things go through my mind. I had no clue. Indi's recent demeanor and appearance have made me suspicious. I knew Indi was in a love mode. That was not difficult to detect. But Rachel? No way! Yet it all now makes sense. It was no coincidence that Jade's card and note came on the heels of Indi's new relationship with Rachel. Since Rachel had been one of Jade's best friends and had spent a lot of time with Jade just prior to her disappearance, it is not difficult to connect the dots. Of course, Rachel would know where to find Jade. She may even have been part of the grand scheme. No wonder Indi was cavalier about Jade's card and note and, as I look back, was the least emotional among us.

"Are you all right?" Mark asks as I begin to shake.

"Hold me," I say. As he holds me tight, I realize that Indi's deception can be viewed as an honorable thing. The family's quest to locate Jade has been foremost in our minds for the past thirty years and clearly the end justifies the means. Indi accomplished something that not even Daddy's money or Mum's prayers were able to accomplish. Indi should be praised rather than condemned. The irrefutable evidence is that Rachel is the intermediary, the messenger who bridges the gap between Jade and our family. It is only through Rachel that unification is possible.

As Mark loosens his grip, I explain to him who Rachel is and the significance of it all. He nods his head in acknowledgment and agrees to keep it all a closely guarded secret. He is accustomed to keeping family secrets he says, apparently for reassurance's sake. I know our secret is safe with Mark and our sharing makes our bond even stronger.

"Speaking of the devil," Mark says as Indi approaches.

"Happy New Year," Indi says as he gives me a firm hug and shakes Mark's hand. "You two look like you have been engaged in serious discussion. Are you finally going to tie the knot?"

"We refuse to answer on the grounds that it may tend to incriminate us," I say flippantly, having regained much of my composure.

"Speaking of pleading the Fifth," Indi says, "I haven't had a drink yet tonight."

"We're right behind you," Mark says.

As I loop my arm through Indi's, I whisper, "We have to talk."

"I was afraid of that," Indi whispers back. "I have a lot to tell you."

While Mark engages in a political discussion with two of the male guests, I pull Indi aside. Fighting back the tears, I say, "You know, your secret would have been safe with me. I can't believe you didn't tell me."

Flushed, Indi responds, "Quite honestly, I didn't know what to do. I made a promise to Rachel I felt I had to keep."

When Indi starts to look away, I grab his forearm, spilling his drink and force him to look me in the eye. "Is Rachel Rachel Jianlei-Josselyn, Jade's and my ex-classmate?" I ask.

Wiping the spill with a napkin, he responds, "One and the same."

"And Rachel is more important than your family?" I ask.

"You don't understand."

"What is there to understand?"

"You don't get it, do you? My intent was to cultivate Rachel's friendship in an effort to locate Jade. It was done with Mom's blessing."

"I am embarrassed by having jumped to conclusions," I say apologetically and place my arms around Indi.

"It's not all honorable," he says as he pushes me away.

"You realize she is a married woman?"

Indi frowns. "Our involvement is not something I had anticipated. It just happened."

"Aren't you flirting with disaster?"

"If it results in Jade's reappearance it will be worth the risk."

"Don't you think you should explore the options?"

As Mark returns, Indi nods and walks away.

JADE

WHAT MUST I HAVE BEEN THINKING when I sent the Christmas card and note to my family? By doing so, I no doubt created the impression that I was content with their years of rejection and oppression and that it was okay to treat me the way they did. Also, didn't I risk being detected and providing hints that would ultimately lead to my discovery?

I will have to admit that two wrongs don't make a right and that because my parents weren't compassionate doesn't mean that I should not be forgiving and compassionate. Withholding my love for over thirty years may be considered overkill in some quarters. Certainly, both Rachel and Adrien think so. Their argument is that the acts and omissions I consider the most egregious were indirect and unintentional; those acts and omissions for which I am responsible have been direct and deliberate. No quarrel there. There is always a day of reckoning and, for that I should feel guilty?

When I sent my card and note, there was that moment of hesitation. And, after it was irretrievable, there was that moment of relief. My misgivings since, I have concluded, are irrational in light of my true feelings at the time the words were penned. I have exaggerated the justification for my misery as well as the amount of harm caused by the acts of those who thought they were doing the right thing. Then again, isn't the harm the same whether it was intentional or inadvertent?

I go full circle when I place myself in my parents' situation and then plead my case. I often find myself doing a complete turnaround. Playing both roles places everything in perspective, at least when looking through the eyes of the one initiating the action. Being on the receiving end, however, presents its own particular problem and that is determining justification. Its subjectivity is what makes it elusive.

Rachel has sent me a treasure trove of memorabilia chronicling the events of my family for the past thirty years. It compares the then with the now. The contrast is striking. The time lapse portrays the fragility and vulnerability of humankind and the fact that longevity is as elusive as a gust of wind. I will have to admit that Mum and Daddy have not aged well and that it is apparent that their days are numbered. Crimson and I look the way I remember Mum looking when she was our age. Indi looks more like Daddy looked when I left home. Mum was forty-five and Daddy was forty-nine. Today Crimson and I are three years older than Mum was back then and one year younger than Daddy was. I guess everything is relative. It pains me to think that Mum is now seventy-six and Daddy will be eighty in another month. There is no way to recoup the thirty years that have been lost because of my impetuosity. I have been impervious to their feelings and only hope they will find it in their hearts to forgive.

"Hey, why so somber?" Adrien says as he enters the room.

"Just going through some of the items Rachel sent me," I say. "They bring back some memories and some regrets."

"We all make mistakes," Adrien says.

"If I could undo some of it, I would—all except being with you, that is."

"Do you realize that in less than two months we will have been married thirty years?"

"Hard to believe. It seems only like yesterday that destiny brought us together."

"I thought you said it was the stars or the positioning of the planets that brought us together."

"It was preordained. That is all I can tell you. Are you sorry you got tangled up with the twin whose tattoo bespoke doom?"

"You know how I feel about you. Nothing could make me change my mind about you, especially not the configuration of the symbol on your right ankle." With that Adrien gently rolls down my anklet and reverently kisses me on the storied tattoo.

As Adrien scrutinizes the photographs of my parents, he laments the automobile accident that claimed the lives of his parents the proceeding summer. "Nothing good came of it," he says.

"We wouldn't be in this beautiful townhouse overlooking the landmarks of Paris if it hadn't been for your parents," I say. Then I quickly add, "Not that we would trade any of this for their lives. They were more like parents to me than my own parents."

"That's because you allowed them to be," Adrien replies. "When you reached out, they gave you their hearts. They could not have loved you more and did everything within their power to make sure you fulfilled your dreams."

"My parents were like that once," I say.

"They still are," Adrien says. "All you have to do is reach out."

"You don't understand," I say to Adrien. His eyes tell me he doesn't and probably never will.

"Don't you miss your parents?" he asks.

"More so than ever before," I reply. "Knowing they will not be around much longer makes it more imperative than ever that we reconcile our differences. However, I have lived without them for thirty years and done well without their interference. Don't you think I can continue to do so?"

"Let me answer it this way. I didn't quite live up to my parents' expectations, especially my father's. He envisioned I would be some kind of tennis star or other professional. Being a computer programmer for a medical clinic was not something he had in mind. Even though I failed him, he still professed to be proud of me. Regardless of my successes or failures, I knew my parents were interested and that they were available to share my accomplishments and failures. With them gone, there is an emptiness that I can't quite describe."

"You can share with me and also your sister."

"You miss my point. Your parents are still alive and you choose not to honor them by making them proud. They have no idea that you've completed nursing training and are a registered nurse. Nor are they sure you're proficient in two languages. You have made a name for yourself in the medical field, something usually reserved for the specialists. You make more money than I do."

"I don't know how being a nurse would be for my father. He would only be satisfied if I were a brain surgeon or forensic psychiatrist. He has told me as much."

"You're selling yourself short and you're cheating your parents by not keeping them involved. I implore you not to squander the opportunity. Place yourself in their position. They brought you into this world, nurtured you for eighteen years and gave you opportunities afforded very few. For thirty years they haven't known whether you were dead or alive. Is that the kind of payback they deserve?"

"I'm concerned it's too late. I know they cancelled my credit cards when I left and I'm not sure whether or not they have disinherited me. When they die everything will probably go to Indi and Crimson."

"Get real. If you were your parents, who would you reward, the ones who stayed behind and devoted their lives to you or the one who tormented you with deception, defection and dishonor?"

"You make me sound like a monster. I thought you liked me."

"I love you. That's why I want you to do the right thing so that you will be at peace, especially at peace with yourself. Why is that so difficult for you to understand?"

"I don't think it's fair for Indi and Crimson to inherit my parents' estate. If I had children, they would all get an equal share. How would you have felt if Vivienne had inherited everything?"

"I've never considered I had any entitlements to something I had not earned. The inheritance from my parents is a windfall and not something I counted on or ever expected. I would gladly trade it all to see them one more time."

PART SEVEN

TRIAL
AND
ERROR

CRIMSON

"HOW ARE YOU FEELING ?" Corkey asks.

"In a word, humiliated," I respond as I position myself at the defense table, this time not in the role as an attorney but in my new role as defendant. Even though I am uncuffed and in civilian attire, I am still under the watchful eye and the charge of the uniformed jail matron who is positioned inside the rail not far behind me.

Presiding over my trial will be Judge Gretchen Farrington. She was two classes ahead of me at the USF School of Law and also obtained her undergraduate degree at Stanford before me. The two of us served together on several committees for the California Bar Association, including the Criminal Law Section. How ironic it is, I think, that the two of us would be using our legal training and experience in this fashion.

As we wait for Judge Farrington to appear, I think back three months earlier when I was arrested for the death of my brother Indi. I found him lying on the kitchen floor bleeding from a wound to the chest. Mark had just dropped me off after we attended church together and then went to brunch at his parents' home not far from ours. It was early afternoon.

In a panic, I tried to revive Indi and couldn't. He was cool to the touch and I could find no vital signs. It was unclear as to what happened and when but it was clear that Indi was dead. According to the dispatcher's record, I called 911 on that fateful Sunday afternoon in May, 2007, at one fifty-eight p.m.

I impulsively tried to put the pieces together as to what had occurred as I awaited the arrival of the EMTs. In the process of trying to revive Indi, I had pushed a blood-stained knife aside, obliterating any fingerprints that may have been on it and had soaked up a fair amount of Indi's blood as I knelt beside him. Although I didn't realize it at the time, I left my fingerprints on the knife, a weapon that later was determined to have caused Indi's death.

Rachel arrived shortly after the EMTs arrived and, seeing me crying and covered in blood, understandably concluded, or at least so it appeared to me, that I was responsible for Indi's death. That was obvious from what I detected in her eyes and from her abrupt withdrawal as I attempted to approach her. An hour earlier, one of the next-door neighbors allegedly saw Indi and me standing in front of the sliding glass doors leading to the back deck engaged in what he described to the police as a heated debate. My only look-alike would have been Jade, whom we have not seen or heard from directly for over thirty years. Regardless, I know it wasn't me.

"Sorry for the delay," Judge Farrington says as she calls the case of *People of the State of California versus*

Crimson Ziang. "The court had an emergency matter that required attention," she announces.

After determining that both sides are ready, she asks Marianne Woodly, the chief prosecutor for the district attorney's office for the City and County of San Francisco, if the prosecution is ready to make its opening statement.

"The prosecution is ready," Marianne says. Marianne had been a prosecuting attorney with the same office at the same time as me but had made it a career. I was surprised she would take on my case in light of our prior affiliation. She is in her early sixties and is not at all attractive and wasn't even in her earlier days when I first knew her. Her features suggest a calloused and insensitive prosecutor who is case hardened and unyielding. There are many battle-scarred defense attorneys who flinch when her name is mentioned and will unquestionably vouch for her tenacity.

Marianne, who has been aggressive in seeking my conviction on first-degree murder charges, is quick out of the gate.

"We are here to seek justice against a cold-blooded killer," she says, "one who didn't even hold sacred the life of her own brother and who even today as she sits here shows no remorse. The evidence in this case will show that Crimson Ziang, the defendant, with premeditation, deliberation and malice aforethought on Sunday, May 27, 2007, at approximately one o'clock p.m., at the family home, violently attacked and stabbed the victim, Indigo Ziang, thus causing her own brother's death.

"The prosecution will show beyond a reasonable doubt that Ms. Ziang had the motive, opportunity and means to commit the murder. Her motive was greed. Both of her parents had recently passed and she wasn't at all satisfied with her brother administering their parents' estate or him being named trustee. Also, she felt that her brother had received a disproportionate share of their parents' estate. As for opportunity, she and her brother lived, and for all their lives had lived, secluded in a mansion in one of the exclusive areas of San Francisco. Their nearest neighbor was at least a half football field away. Her false security, however, led to her undoing as the closest neighbor, Conrad Middleton, who will be called as a witness, observed Ms. Ziang and her brother embroiled in what appeared to be a heated argument less than an hour before she stabbed him. The means, of course, will be introduced as an exhibit. It is a rather imposing kitchen knife, a lethal weapon capable of inflicting grievous bodily injury and, of course, the cause of her brother's death.

"How do we prove Ms. Ziang is the one who committed the murder, other than that she had motive, opportunity and means? Well, that is not as difficult as it sounds. Ms. Ziang was seen engaged, as I mentioned, in a heated argument with her brother less than an hour before his death. He was alive then. The next time he is seen, he is dead. When the EMTs arrive, they observe Ms. Ziang in close proximity to the body, covered in blood. Ms. Ziang's fingerprints are later found on the murder weapon along with some of her own blood and, of course, the blood of the victim.

"You will be aided by both direct and circumstantial evidence in this case. The finger of guilt you will soon learn points directly at Ms. Ziang. With the overwhelming evidence we anticipate will be presented, you should have no difficulty in returning a guilty verdict."

I am gripped with sorrow when I think of my parents' death and now the death of my brother. Mum died on Sunday, February 18, 2007, just as she had predicted. Daddy died less than two months later on April 8, 2007, again a Sunday. Sunday being the Lord's day makes me wonder if it was more than a coincidence that Mum, Daddy and Indi all died on the same day of the week; and, all within such a short period of time.

"Mr. Whittaker, do you wish to make an opening statement at this time?" Judge Farrington asks.

"We elect to reserve it until the conclusion of the state's case," Corkey responds.

"Very well then. The prosecution may proceed with its case."

Marianne calls as her first witness the dispatcher for 911 who testifies as to the call from me reporting Indi's death. The next two witnesses are the EMTs who testify as to the condition of Indi's body, his state of being, my bloody clothing, the bloody knife and removal of Indi's body. It is all so matter of fact. To them, Indi is just another statistic.

The county coroner and pathologist testify as to Indi's state of being. They attribute the cause of death as being a severed aorta, the positioning of the entry wound, the likelihood the wound was caused by the knife found at the scene and the absence of any other wounds on Indi's body.

The investigating officers testify as to the crime scene investigation, the collection and preservation of evidence, the crime scene photographs, and identification and chain of custody of the murder weapon.

The lab technicians/analysts testify as to their respective examinations and conclusions and establish that the fingerprints found on the murder weapon were those exclusively belonging to me and no one else in the world, that the blood found on the murder weapon belonged to both Indi and me, and that the blood on my clothing and on the floor of the crime scene belonged to Indi. Corkey was able to elicit admissions on cross-examination that the blood found on the weapon could have come from an identical twin such as Jade since both DNAs would be virtually the same. They admitted they couldn't exclude Jade as the source for the blood that had been attributed as having come from me.

Questionable evidence also came from a handwriting expert who analyzed my mother's diary. Some weeks before Mum's death, she had scribbled in her diary next to February 28th the notation "Chenzoi's departure from earth—4:25 a.m." On April 8, 2007, which was Easter Sunday, she penned "Lanzu's departure from earth—10:46 a.m." On May 27, 2007, the day Indi died and the day before Memorial Day, she noted "Day Indi will make his journey to his heavenly home—1:00 p.m."

It's common knowledge that both Mum's handwriting and mine were similar. The authorities discounted the possibility that Mum could have forecast her own date and time of death or that of Daddy's and Indi's. *The dead don't journal their own deaths* they told the court at our suppression hearing. The prosecution agreed that the notations were made by someone long before their happenings, at least as far as Indi's notation was concerned. They were placed there more likely than not, according to the prosecution, by me. They speculated that I had placed the three entries in Mum's journal *after* my parents' deaths and *before* Indi's. It is proof, according to them, that Indi's death, therefore, was deliberate and premeditated.

Because the state's handwriting expert could not say for certain that the handwriting was not mine and that it was possible if not probable that the entries were made by me, the evidence was allowed to be introduced even over our objection. The jurors were given the cautionary instruction that they could give the evidence whatever weight they deemed was warranted. This was Judge Farrington's chicken way out of having made a bad ruling.

"I can't believe Farrington allowed such specu-lative evidence," I whisper to Corkey. I see Judge Farrington glare at me with pinched eyebrows. I was hoping she hadn't overheard my comment.

"In the event of conviction," Corkey whispers back, "it could bolster our chances of a reversal on appeal."

A lot of consolation, I think as I make a mental assessment of my chances of acquittal in light of all the prejudicial circumstantial evidence presented, especially the questionable evidence Judge Farrington didn't have the guts to exclude.

"It is our turn to go on the offense," Corkey says as the jury recesses for the week.

That following Monday, Corkey is poised to make his opening statement in my behalf. Cordell Desmond Whittaker was District Attorney of the City and County of San Francisco at the time I gradu-ated from law school in 1985. It was Corkey who hired me when I was still wet behind the ears. All my trial skills I learned from Corkey. When he left office in 1990, I did likewise and it was shortly thereafter that I was hired on by Cantaberry, Brussels, Hanover & Greenberg.

Corkey is not physically imposing but intellectu-ally he is a giant. At age sixty-six he is still the litigator you hire when you are in trouble. It has long been said that when you want the best you hire Corkey.

However, his representation comes with a price. There are no coupons or discounts to help defray the fees. But he is worth every cent.

Corkey's style is deceptive. He'll try to kill you with kindness and if that doesn't work, he will beat you to death. He is a brilliant tactician with a golden tongue and can charm the socks off you. At least that is the way Mark and the others in our firm have described him. Corkey, for whatever reason, has refused a retainer or any payment of any sort from me. I know that I will find a way to repay him. Since my arrest, he and his staff are the only ones I can depend on. Without Corkey, I would be adrift in a sea of despair without so much as even a paddle.

"Ladies and gentlemen of the jury," Corkey begins, "no doubt some of you are ready to convict even though you have not heard all the evidence. Even though Crimson Ziang is not required to testify, which is the right of every person accused of a crime in our country, she feels she owes it to you to do so.

"We anticipate that the evidence will show the following. Crimson and her sister Jade are identical twins. Identical twins, though their fingerprints are different, have the same DNA. It is possible, therefore, that the blood found at the scene not belonging to Indi could have come from Crimson's sister Jade.

"Crimson will admit to having removed the knife thought to be the so-called murder weapon so as to render aid to her brother. More likely than not then, the knife would contain her fingerprints. She will also testify that the knife was part of a set that she used on a daily basis to prepare meals for the family. She will confirm that she did not wear rubber gloves when she handled the kitchen utensils either while cooking, setting the table or doing dishes.

"On the day of the terrible tragedy, Crimson arose early so as to be ready when her fiancé picked her up for church at seven-thirty a.m. and didn't arrive back home until sometime around one fifty p.m. Not only will she be testifying to that but so will her fiancé. Not being there, it is obvious that the female seen at the scene arguing with Indi was not her. She has a sister with identical features and Indi had a lady friend about his sisters' age. Crimson will tell you she rarely argued with her brother and never were they even close to being violent. She will refute the notion that the two argued on the day of Indi's death. In fact, the last time she saw Indi was ten p.m. on the previous evening.

"Crimson will deny ever having made any entries in her mother's diary. Even after her mother's death, she will testify she never handled the diary. It was left on her mother's nightstand right where her mother had placed it. She doubts that her father even touched it as the family respected the mother's privacy and the diary was considered a shrine of sorts.

"Through cross-examination and the evidence presented by the defense, you will come to the ines-capable conclusion that Indigo Ziang's death was an accident and not a murder. If you conclude it was a murder, then you will find that it was not perpetrated by the sister who idolized him."

I was called as the first defense witness and described our family history and the makeup of the family, the loving relationship we all had with one and other, the special relationship I had with my brother, the absence of jealously between the two of us, the absence of any motive to want my brother dead, my alibi, and my refutation of the various prosecution allegations. Corkey felt I had withstood Marianne's vitriolic attacks, accusations and innuendoes in an admirable fashion. I felt good about my testimony and its effect on the jury. As Corkey used to say, it's easy when you're telling the truth.

The next witness we call is my ex-fiancé, Mark. I say my *ex* because even though I still wear his ring I am uncertain we are still engaged. After my arrest and denial of a bond, I saw Mark rarely and we both agreed to put everything on hold pending the outcome of the prosecution. It is obvious he is conflicted by family pressure. He admits his family has persuaded him to distance himself from me in an effort to preserve their family name. I understand that and am content to let nature take its course.

As Mark is sworn in and takes the witness stand, our eyes meet. In his eyes I still see love; on his brow I see worry. This is a terrible thing I have put him through. Not only have I been an embarrassment to the firm but to him and the entire Cantaberry family as well. I am nervous, but not as nervous as Mark. Neither of us has been placed in this position before. I know he is eager to help me and hope he will emotionally be up to the task. His greatest asset is his integrity and he is the only one who can substantiate my alibi defense.

Mark traces the sequence of events as they unfolded from the time he picked me up at my home at seven-thirty a.m. until the time he dropped me off at my front door at around two p.m. or thereabouts. He testified as to our attending church service together, eating brunch with his parents and later driving around the downtown area of San Francisco. In response to Corkey's question as to how I appeared on that date, Mark responded, "Her usual loveable self. If anything was bothering her, I didn't detect it. I was scheduled to return to have dinner with Crimson and Indi at six that night and we were all planning to go to a movie together afterwards. Indi was a tennis buddy and the three of us often did things together. When we were short a player, my sister Colette would sometimes join us to complete a foursome. In fact, the reason we didn't play tennis that afternoon was because we couldn't recruit a fourth player, as Colette was spending the weekend with our cousins in Oakland."

Marianne had been fairly gentle with me during cross-examination so as not to antagonize the jury. With Mark, however, it was a different story. Her bulldog side erupted when she didn't get the

responses from him that she wanted. She soon
resorted to the tactics she learned at the baby prosecutor's school and after having tried too many cases
with public defenders.

"Now you're engaged to Crimson Ziang, the
defendant in this case, is that right?"

"Yes."

"And you love her very much. Don't you?"

Even though he was not a litigator, Mark was
wise as to what Marianne's next question would be so
he beat her to the punch.

"Yes," he answered and then quickly added, "but
not enough to lie for her."

Marianne grimaced and scrambled to ask another
question.

"When you said you dropped the defendant off at
her front door, you didn't actually go inside, did you?"

"No."

"Then you don't know for certain whether Indi
was alive or dead when the defendant arrived at the
home, do you?"

"No, except only by what Crimson told me later."

"Sir, my question is whether *you* knew based on
your own personal knowledge."

"My answer is no."

"Before you answer my next question, think
about it carefully. Are you certain it was around two
p.m. when you dropped the defendant off at the front
door?"

Without hesitation, Mark responds, "Yes."

"I told you to think about it before you responded."

"I don't have to," he says, "I know it was around two when I dropped Crimson off."

"Ah-h-h-h!" Marianne says shaking her finger at Mark. "If you knew the exact time, you would have stated it, knowing how important the time factor is in this case. Am I right?"

"Yes."

"So let's get it straight. You didn't look at your watch and, therefore, don't know for certain what the time was. Am I correct?"

"I didn't look at my watch because I didn't have reason to. Time was not of the essence. And, yes, I don't know for certain."

"Crimson, during her testimony, said she arrived home at approximately one fifty p.m. which is, according to my calculations, ten minutes earlier than what you testified to. Am I again correct?"

"I assume that's what she testified to since she told me the same thing. And, yes, that is ten minutes earlier than I remembered."

"Okay. Let's go at this another way. Since you don't know the exact time, couldn't you have delivered Crimson home an hour earlier than you remembered?"

"That's possible but that would be contrary to my recollection."

"Just so I understand your answer here today under oath. It is possible you could have dropped

Crimson off at her home as early as one p.m. Is that your testimony?"

"That possibly could have been the time but I don't think so."

I could hear Marianne snicker as she announced to the court that she had no other questions of the witness. I could tell by the faces of the jurors that Marianne's cross-examination had its intended effect.

Corkey reached over and scribbled on my legal pad. "It's not over till it's over. Don't lose heart yet." I was unable to manage even a smile in return and avoided eye-contact with Mark as he left the courtroom.

We call our own handwriting expert who contradicts the testimony of the expert called by the prosecution. He states that it is his opinion that the entries in Mum's diary were made by no one other than Mum. Although Mum's and my handwriting are similar, he testifies, they are not the same. Marianne asks in her typical sarcastic fashion, "Do you realize that your testimony makes Chenzoi Ziang a clairvoyant?"

Dr. Roddenhoff is unflappable. "Whether or not Chenzoi Ziang is a clairvoyant I can't, with any authority, answer. But I can, with authority, tell you that the entries in her diary were not made by the defendant."

Corkey, who tries to stifle a smile, reaches over and scribbles on my legal pad, "Start believing!"

My optimism is buoyed by Dr. Roddenhoff's testimony and that of our next witness. Lydia Burney,

Corkey's investigator, who presents a video of the sliding glass doors leading from the kitchen to the back deck. It was shot near the Middleton's back wall where Conrad Middleton claims he had seen Indi and I engaged in a heated argument. When Conrad testified for the prosecution, one would question his vision as he was constantly shoving his pop-bottle-like glasses to the bridge of his nose with his right index finger, as they kept sliding down. His demeanor was not the only thing that was laughable. Lydia, for the video, had two of her cohorts stand directly behind the sliding glass doors at about the same time of the day Conrad claims he saw Indi and me arguing. The video revealed not even a silhouette. Both the prosecution and Conrad apparently forgot that the windows were tinted.

This time, Corkey writes on my legal pad, "What a difference a few witnesses make!" I nod my acquiescence and this time manage a smile.

At our request, Judge Farrington takes a short recess. Although we are ready to rest our case-in-chief, we take this time to make sure there are no other witnesses to be called. We opt not to call Rachel as she refused to be interviewed and her testimony would only reinforce what the EMTs had already testified to. So, when the court reconvenes, Corkey announces that the defense rests.

When Marianne announces that the prosecution rests without presenting rebuttal, both Corkey and I are surprised. We thought they would call Rachel, who would have testified as having seen me distraught and covered in blood standing next to Indi's body. As Judge Farrington is engaged in a sidebar with one of the clerks, Corkey looks at me and whispers, "The prosecution must have had the same problem as the defense in corralling Rachel. She truly is a recalcitrant witness."

"She wouldn't have added much anyway," I reply. "The EMTs have already established I was covered with Indi's blood when they arrived on the scene."

"Don't you think maybe Rachel was protecting someone?" Corkey asks.

"What do you mean?" I ask.

"I hear that Dr. Josselyn is not a man to be trifled with. If he found out that Indi was having an affair with his wife, he might not be very understanding and forgiving. What's that old adage? You live by the sword; you die by the sword!"

"There is also an old Chinese proverb," I say, "that goes something like this. A wise man does not play with another man's wife; a lucky man is one who does not get caught."

When Corkey was talking about Rachel protecting someone, Jade's face flashed on the screen of my mind briefly but long enough for me to wonder. After all, if anyone would know if Jade were in town, it would be Rachel. And that look on Rachel's face when she saw me draped in Indi's blood still haunts me. I wondered if maybe she thought I was Jade.

Just at that moment, Judge Farrington breaks

the sidebar with her clerk and announces, "My clerk tells me I have clear sledding first thing tomorrow morning. I can meet with counsel at eight a.m. in chambers and we can get started on finalizing the instructions. Are both counsel available at that time?" Both Marianne and Corkey answer in the affirmative and the jury is excused until eight a.m. on Monday, at which time they are told the attorneys will be presenting their final arguments.

By noon on Friday, Judge Farrington has made her rulings on the tendered instructions to the jury and both the prosecution and the defense are provided with copies. The instructions will be given to the jury prior to their deliberations and contain the principles of law applicable to the case.

Surprisingly, Marianne's opening argument was brief.

"Don't return a guilty verdict to first degree murder because I have asked for it but because it is warranted. And, if you find Crimson Ziang guilty of first degree murder, don't recommend the death penalty because I have asked for it, but again because it is warranted.

"What made Cain's murder of Abel so egregious was not the murder of another but the murder of one's brother. Crimson Ziang had blood on her hands when she murdered her brother Indi and she has blood on her hands now. She had the motive, the opportunity and the means. And now, you ladies and gentlemen of the jury have the motive, the opportunity and the means to see that justice is done by returning a guilty verdict. There is no mark on Crimson's head to prevent the death penalty from being imposed as there was in Cain's situation and to impose it in this case is clearly justified. You, however, will be making that determination, as the court advised you during jury selection, at the penalty phase of the trial and only after you have returned a guilty verdict."

Even the jurors appeared surprised at the brevity of Marianne's argument. But Marianne had made her points. Now it was Corkey's turn.

"Serving on a death penalty case is not an easy one. In biblical times it was an eye for an eye, a tooth for a tooth. If you took someone's life, you paid the penalty by forfeiting your own life. Hopefully, we've become more humane since the time of Cain and Abel. The difference between Cain and Abel and Crimson and Indi is that Crimson didn't murder Indi. We're not sure anyone did but we know for certain that Indi's death was not caused by Crimson.

"Ms. Woodly has presented you with a beautifully wrapped box adorned with a pretty bow and offers it to you for acceptance. The problem is that when you undo the bow and strip away the fluff, you are left with an empty box, a box with nothing in it. Like the prosecution's case, when you strip away all the trappings, there is nothing left of any substance.

"The prosecution's argument is that Crimson *must* have done it because, when the EMTs arrived, she was covered in blood and the knife she cast away to administer to her brother bore her fingerprints. Never mind that her prints may have been placed on the knife when it was used to prepare the meals. And never mind that the blood on the knife, other than Indi's, could have come from Crimson's identical twin, inasmuch as Crimson bore no wounds of any kind. If there were any, the matron at the station house where she was booked in would most certainly have found them during the strip search and that fact would have been iterated and reiterated *ad nauseam* during the course of this trial.

"Consider the message you will be sending if you return a guilty verdict in this case as requested by the prosecution. That message is this. Think twice about helping someone in distress, especially if that someone is a brother or sister, because if you by chance get blood on your hands or clothing and leave fingerprints behind, you in all likelihood will be prosecuted for murder if that person dies and can't vouch for you.

"No wonder our society has evolved to the point where there is a reluctance to come to another's aid or rescue for fear of becoming the prime suspect, or of being sued by the person rescued because you hadn't performed all the procedures dictated by twenty-twenty hindsight. Never mind that you were not medically trained or medically savvy or that you, through haste and panic, did or didn't do what a jury such as yourselves would have done or not have done after hours of deliberation, discussion and careful consideration.

"There is one thing upon which the prosecution and defense agree and that is that with the case being turned over to you ladies and gentlemen you now have the motive, opportunity and means to see that justice is done. However, unlike Ms. Woodly, we are asking that you not convict an innocent woman for a crime she didn't commit. Actually, the test is not whether Crimson Ziang is innocent but whether the prosecution has provided sufficient evidence to convince you of her guilt beyond a reasonable doubt. We submit that they have not and that you are, therefore, bound by law to come back with a *not guilty* verdict. And, that is what we are asking you to do."

When Marianne rises to deliver the prosecution's closing argument, I can tell by her gait, her tilt of the head and her sly grin that I better brace myself. Corkey's scribble on the slip of paper he sets on the top of my legal pad reads, "Prepare yourself by taking a deep breath and letting the air out slowly. Woodly is on the warpath and takes no prisoners."

It is not long before I realize that it probably will all have been in vain and that Marianne will have her way in the end.

With typical Woodly flare, Marianne inches her face to the closest point of the podium facing the jury and with her arms folded in stubborn determination systematically engages the eyes of each and every juror including the alternates. After methodically retracing her gaze, she speaks in a hushed tone.

"I can see in each of your eyes," she begins, "that you have not been taken in by defense counsel's clever and creative rhetoric. Remember *rhetoric is not reason and emotion is not evidence*. In effect, Mr. Whittaker is asking you to find that the world is flat, that water is not wet and that wrong is right. Your eyes tell me you are not about to buy, let alone swallow, Mr. Whittaker's snake oil.

"When I was a child, I remember getting into my mother's jewelry box, which was a no-no, and, in the process of trying on several of her necklaces, I happened to unravel a strand of priceless pearls. They rolled all over the floor and some I held in my hand as she walked in the door. As I stood there wearing several necklaces, including the one with the broken strand, my mother asked what I was doing in her jewelry box. 'I wasn't' I said, with a straight face and looking at her directly in the eye. As she surveyed the scene, she said, 'You don't really expect me to believe that, now do you?' My redemption was in coming clean and admitting my error. In her eyes, I had sinned twice, once was by flouting the rules, the other, and the one most egregious, at least to her, was me lying about my involvement despite the overwhelming evidence to the contrary.

"In the case before you, Crimson Ziang was caught with her hand in the cookie jar, so to speak, much as was I. She has committed a heinous crime in violation of California law. When she was seen arguing with her brother less than one hour before his death and seen covered in her brother's blood less than two hours later, and the murder weapon found bearing her fingerprints, she still lied about her involvement and was able to take the stand under oath and, with a straight face and looking each of you directly in the eyes, as I did moments ago, deny she had killed her brother in cold blood.

"I have been prosecuting cases a long time but I've never been involved in a case where the defendant confessed to a crime before it happened. The diary of the defendant's mother is one of the exhibits you will be allowed to take into the jury room during your deliberations. The entries in the diary of the deaths of defendant's mother and father were mere historical accounts. The entry of the death of the victim in this case, which was made as were the other two by the defendant, was not a prediction or lucky guess as the defense would have you believe, but a carefully scripted scheme, evincing deliberation and premeditation, to end her brother's life.

"So what kind of evidence has the prosecution presented to support the act, the intent and the premeditation in this case? You have direct evidence, you have circumstantial evidence and you have what is tantamount to a confession. Normally, the prosecution is able to present only one or maybe two but seldom all three as we have in this case.

"As I conclude my final argument, I need to remind you that Crimson Ziang is not just any defendant and the murder is not just any murder. Crimson Ziang has been trained in the law and can't claim ignorance of the law, which is not a valid defense anyway. She is a licensed attorney and at one time was a prosecuting attorney just like me. She is intimately familiar with the law and especially criminal law. She knew what she was doing when she planned her brother's death, she knew what she was doing when she killed him, she knew what she was doing when she engaged in the phony cover up, and she knows, as she sits here today, what the probable outcome of this trial will be. When I said this was not just any murder, I had reference to the killing of one's own brother. This is something you will be called upon to consider at the penalty phase of the trial after you have returned your *guilty* verdict."

Marianne's plea to the jury was textbook perfect. Even I wanted to find myself guilty and "hang the bastard." But to do so would be to convict an innocent person. And that is something no jury should ever do.

My whole future is in the hands of the jury. Twelve persons tried and true who know me not will be determining my fate. And, if they find me guilty, will be recommending whether I live or die. My whole life is condensed into a few short weeks and my future determined in a few short hours. I am too numb to worry and too distraught to muster hope. In some ways I just want it over. One way or the other, I want it over. The last four months have been the longest of my life. Being denied bail and being locked up made me appreciate what my favorite pet, Fuzzy, endured as a domesticated rabbit while his contemporaries roamed free. Freedom is appreciated only after it has been taken away.

The jury is out less than four hours when the bailiff is advised they have reached a verdict. "Some kind of record for a capital case," Corkey says as the jury is ushered into the courtroom. We agree that is a good sign for the defense. Still my hopes remain stagnant. My years as an attorney have taught me that jurors are unpredictable and fickle and that they can arrive at the right decision for the wrong reason or the wrong decision without any reason.

My heart is in my throat as the bailiff hands the written verdict form to the judge. Corkey squeezes my hand and says nothing. I can tell by his clammy hands that he is apprehensive and tentative. Both of us hold our breaths as Judge Farrington reads, "We the jury duly empanelled and sworn do find the defendant, Crimson Ziang . . ." She hesitates long enough for my heart to stop beating. As she looks up from the form and directly at me she concludes, ". . .guilty as charged."

The next thing I know Corkey, with the assistance of the bailiff and my assigned matron, are helping me to my chair and handing me a glass of water. "Did I hear right?" I manage to whisper to Corkey. I can see that he has not taken the verdict well, either.

Later he will confess to me he thought we would emerge victorious.

"That is the first murder case I have lost as either a prosecutor or a defense attorney and it had to happen in your case," he says. We both fight back the tears and, out of the corner of my eyes, I can see Marianne high-fiving her investigator and advisory witness. She gloats as she adds another notch to her belt.

Corkey dispatches his investigator to speak to the jurors who were disposed to talk. Lydia reported later that they said that my having been seen arguing with Indi just prior to his death, my being covered in Indi's blood when the EMTs arrived, my fingerprints being found on the handle of the murder weapon, and my journal entry foretelling Indi's death, along with Mark's uncertainty as to when he drove me home on the day of Indi's death, are what persuaded them that I was Indi's killer. Apparently, when the jury took the straw vote there was no disagreement. With me having been a prosecuting attorney, they felt I was desensitized and that my lack of emotion in the courtroom was proof of my insensitivity and lack of remorse.

How could I show remorse, if I hadn't done anything wrong? How could Conrad Middleton have seen me through tinted glass doors, especially since I wasn't there at the time? How could I be convicted for journal entries I never made? If I had been the perpetrator, why would I have called 911 and stayed around and waited for the police to arrive? Why had the authorities spent all their time and resources building a case against me and not exploring the possibility of alternate suspects? Why did the district attorney's office refuse to accept the polygraph results of their own polygrapher showing that I was telling the truth when I denied any involvement in the death of my brother? I could go on and on but my musings lead nowhere and only point out what Jade has preached for years: *There is no such thing as justice!*

On Tuesday, at eight a.m., we are scheduled for the penalty phase of my trial. It is a time when the jury will decide whether to recommend either life imprisonment or death by lethal injection. The prosecution will argue for the death penalty. We will argue for a life sentence. If the jury recommends the death penalty, Judge Farrington will decide to either reject or accept the recommendation and I will be sentenced accordingly.

It is a long weekend that I spend incarcerated and unable to find any peace. There is no expectation that my prayers will be answered. In many respects the death penalty would probably be more tolerable than being imprisoned for the rest of my life without the possibility of parole. When I think about it, I really have no reason to live. Things can only be better on the other side.

Even with the recommendation of the probation department, evidence of my impeccable record, and the favorable polygraph results which were inadmissible at the trial phase, the jury recommends the death penalty. Marianne argues for the death penalty; Corkey asks for leniency. When Judge Farrington asks if I have anything to say before imposing sentence, I stand and pray for divine inspiration and intercession so that I can make the most persuasive argument of my life. Only this time, *my* life depends on it.

"If the son of God was unable to save himself when he was falsely accused of something he hadn't done, then how can I? And, if his heavenly father had not interceded so that the son could atone for the sins of mankind, then how can I expect our heavenly father to intercede for me? I question not the reason I have been falsely accused, placed on trial, and unjustly convicted but have faith that the almighty has a reason and a plan.

"On the basis of the appearances, I find no fault with the prosecution or the decision the jury has reached, nor do I question the motive Your Honor may have in whatever sentence you impose. I know you all think you are doing the right thing. Sometimes, when we think we are doing the right thing, however, we are wrong. All of us have to be guided by our conscience.

"No matter what you may think, I did not cause my brother's death. I have and will always have great love for my brother. My parents have taught us from as far back as I can remember to thine own self be true. To confess to something I didn't do would be to perpetrate a fraud. To be remorseful for something I didn't do would be hypocritical. To beg for mercy for something I didn't do would be to demean my very existence. And to attempt to convince you to change your mind would only unduly delay the inevitable."

Judge Farrington totally disregards the recommendation of the probation department and succumbs to the recommendation of the jury. After all, they are the voice of the people she serves. I am, therefore, sentenced to death by lethal injection.

JADE

I HAD BEEN TOSSING AND TURNING since midnight and had barely fallen asleep when I am awakened by the persistent ring of the telephone. The telephone is on Adrien's side of the bed so he answers. I look at the digital clock on the bed stand next to me. It is two a.m.

"It's for you," Adrien says in the midst of a yawn.

I know it's Rachel before I answer. I can tell it's not good news when I hear Rachel's sobs. She is uncontrollable and unable to speak.

"You don't need to tell me," I say. "Crimson has been sentenced to death." Even though I said it, I can't believe it.

Rachel regains her composure long enough to utter words that cause me to reel.

"Crimson didn't do it," she blurts. "I know who did."

"Oh, my God," I say as I find it difficult to breath. After uncomfortable seconds, she says, "It was Miles. He has a terrible temper, you know. How he knew about Indi and me I have no idea. I just know that somehow he found out."

That isn't at all what I expected to hear and breathe a sigh of relief.

"That's something I would keep to myself," I say. "Without proof, you risk ruining Miles' good name and reputation, his and your lives and, of course, your marriage. I'm pleased that we are good enough friends to confide in one another. But to say anything about this to anyone else would not be a good idea."

After I hang up the telephone and relate the terrible news to Adrien, I find little peace the rest of the night. I am haunted by the events surrounding Indi's death.

I had arrived at San Francisco International Airport on a direct flight from Paris late afternoon Saturday, May 26, 2007. I was scheduled to stay with Rachel and Miles in their home less than thirty minutes from our family home and was met at the airport by Rachel. She had helped me hatch a plan to surprise Crimson on our forty-ninth birthday. Indi was part of the plot and through Rachel we had arranged for me to meet Indi at our family home the following day at eleven-thirty a.m., a time when Crimson was scheduled to be away until mid-afternoon.

On Sunday, May 27, 2007, driving one of the Josselyn vehicles, I arrived at our family home about five minutes early and was greeted by Indi. We both were elated with the reunion as it had been over thirty years since we had last seen each other. There was no doubt as to who his daddy was. He looked, talked and acted like the younger version of our father. We laughed and cried, sometimes at the same time, as we held on to each other and reminisced about old times. I hadn't realized how much I had missed him and the old family place. Just being there stirred within me a mix of emotions. It was difficult, however, to stifle my resentment.

When Adrien and I had discussed my going back to the States, we agreed it would be a dual-purpose mission. One would be to be with Crimson on our forty-ninth birthday and the other would be, obviously, to claim my rightful inheritance. I had no inkling as to how our parents' estate was to be divided. I assumed, of course, it would be split three ways. I was uncertain about division of our home, Chi-Yen's and the other business properties and enterprises. Money and securities would be easy. Division of the rest I knew would be complicated.

It was pretty much decided that our birthday celebration on May 30 would be a private affair with family intimates, which would include the Josselyns, and that it would be held at the family residence. Indi showed me some of the favors and decorations that had been hidden away in one of the guest rooms. The food items were arranged to be picked up the day before.

Indi fixed one of his patented foot-long Dagwood sandwiches, which he cut in half and served with a generous helping of deli potato salad. He had a pitcher of sun tea brewing on the back deck, which he retrieved and poured into tall glasses crammed with ice. He even seated me at the table.

"I see you've become a gentleman in your old age," I said.

"Had a lot of practice," he said beaming.

Indi had no idea that Rachel had been providing me with a detailed account of even their most intimate escapades. Far be it from me to have let on that I knew what he was talking about. To have done so would have been in bad taste and would have interrupted my information line.

As we were finishing our drinks and I was sampling the pastries Indi had set before me, I asked him how the probate of our parents' estate was going and how the family property was to be divided. He appeared flushed and said he would see if he could resurrect copies of our parents' last wills and testaments, as the originals had been filed with the probate court. While he was doing so, I opened the sliding glass doors that led to the back deck and peered at the still carefully groomed landscape. In the midst of doing so, Indi appeared with copies of Mum's and Daddy's wills.

I could feel my temperature rising before I had finished reading both wills. It was apparent that everything was put in a trust and the income divided equally between Indi and Crimson for a period of five years. At the end of the five year period, the principal would be divided into equal shares between Indi and Crimson, or the survivor if one was then deceased. If neither Indi nor Crimson survived, the principal would go to me if I could be found. Otherwise, the property would pass under the laws of intestacy of the State of California.

The more I thought about it, the more enraged I became. When Indi and I became embroiled in heated argument, we could see we had attracted the attention of one of our neighbors, Conrad Middleton. Realizing we were making a disturbance, we went inside and closed the sliding glass doors.

Once inside, we both calmed down to some extent. When I objected to being not only disenfranchised but disinherited, Indi embarked on this diatribe about me having abandoned the family and leaving Crimson and him to care for our aging parents.

"Where were you all these years when you were needed? Don't you think your defection comes with consequences? After thirty-years without a word from you, not knowing whether you were alive or dead, you now come back after our parents are deceased and want your fair share? Do you really think you are entitled to anything?"

I am standing near the cutting board where Indi had prepared our Dagwood and sliced it in half. I grabbed the sharp butcher knife and pointed it in Indi's direction and remembered saying something like, "Indi, you selfish bastard. I ought to cut your heart out and that way you will be *heartless* not just in name."

When Indi turned around to leave, I said, "Don't you dare walk away. Face me like a man." I was still holding the knife extended in his direction and was only a foot or so away from him when he turned abruptly in my direction, impaling himself on the knife blade. I didn't let go of the handle until after he slumped to the floor. I dropped the knife next to his body as I stood there in shock and horror. I don't know how long I stood there. I just remembered trying to find a pulse and couldn't. Not knowing what to do, I showered in Crimson's bathroom and borrowed some of her clothes. On my way back to Rachel's home, I discarded the bagged, bloody clothing in a dumpster behind a shopping center complex.

Upon reaching Rachel's residence, I lost my composure and made up a story about discovering Indi's body. Rachel became hysterical and I did everything in my power to calm her.

When Rachel calmed down somewhat, she announced that she wanted to be alone and retreated to her bedroom. I went to the guestroom. Within minutes I heard her car reeve up and, peering through the curtains, watched as she drove away. Later I learned she had driven over to our family home to see for herself.

The minute she returned, she hurried to her bedroom and retrieved her cell phone which she said she had left behind. When I entered her bedroom, she was distressed because Miles was not answering his. "He always answers his cell phone," she had said. Then, she said something like, "He's supposed to be playing in a golf tournament today. I hope that's what he's been doing."

Now that I think back, I can see why consternation was written all over her face the afternoon Indi died. She thought Miles had killed Indi.

Though I slept little the night before, I am not the least bit tired. I rose early even though I don't have to be at the clinic until nine. Adrien has just finished his shower and is ready for his coffee.

"Pancakes or french toast?" I ask.

"Just fix me what you fix for yourself," he says.

"I'm not hungry," I reply. "Think I will just have coffee and Danish."

"Sounds good to me, too," he says as he doctors his coffee.

"Too much sugar," I say as I watch him empty two full tablespoons into the cup.

"Just trying to be as sweet as you," he says.

"How can you say that? Since I've come back from the States, even you accuse me of being difficult to live with."

"Speaking of the States, if you are the one who ends up with your parents' property in five years, shouldn't we be thinking about where we want to live? It would be agonizing, would it not, to be traveling back and forth?"

"It all depends on what happens to Crimson and when," I say. "Pray that she receives a reprieve."

PART EIGHT

MOMENT OF
REDEMPTION

CRIMSON

I HAVE BEEN NOTIFIED that my date of execution has been scheduled for November 11, 2011. Curiously enough, it is Remembrance Day, a holiday in Canada and in the United States. For me, Marianne Woodly and the District Attorney's Office, it will indeed be a day of remembrance.

On October 10, 2011, I am summoned to the warden's office and am ushered there by one of the guards post haste. It will disappoint a lot of people if it is a commutation; it will disappoint me if it is a stay.

"Ms. Ziang," Warden Roddenbrink begins in a stern voice, "I have received a communique from a Dr. Borden Luman who is the head surgeon at Rose Medical Centre in Paris, France. Apparently, he has become aware of your scheduled execution and has a patient, actually your sister Jade, who is in need of a kidney transplant. On your intake form, you have indicated your willingness to become an organ donor. He is requesting that just prior to your execution that you provide Jade with one of your kidneys. The fresher the organ, the more likely the success. They, of course, have forwarded a stack of consent forms that need to be executed. Is this something you would still be willing to do?"

My inclination is to correct the misconception of who has the healthy kidney and who doesn't. But, before I can sort it out in my mind, I hear myself say, "If that will prolong someone else's life, I will withstand the pain—especially if it my sister's life that is at stake."

"Dr. Luman has asked that you look over these forms and sign them if you approve and forward them in the mailing folder attached. We, of course, will take care of the transmittal. Dr. Luman has also requested that we provide him with the name of a competent surgeon who can assemble a team of surgeons to perform the required surgery. Dr. Luman said that the required fees would be wired as soon as arrangements were made. With only a month to prepare, we need to expedite the process."

With my impending execution and the short window to effectuate the transfer of my kidney to Jade, I have given my consent to have lethal injection as soon as the surgical process has been completed. Apparently, all the powers that be concur that it would be inhumane to have me endure the pain of surgery, revive me and then give me the lethal injection. I sign all the additional consent forms without reading them and am told the surgical process will commence at five-thirty in the morning on the day of execution.

When they wheel Jade in and begin prepping the two of us for surgery at St. Mary's Hospital, located not far from the prison, I'm surprised to see Jade wearing glasses. Jade had never worn eye glasses before and had always had perfect eyesight, as have I. Before I can comment, Jade asks the nurse in charge if she can have a private moment with me. When the nurse hesitates, Jade says, "We haven't seen each other in thirty years and have just a few private things to say to each other before—" She breaks off before she can say that I will die. She rallies and adds, "It will only take a minute or two."

After the nurse leaves, Jade deftly switches our wrist bands. When she takes off her glasses and sticks them on me, I understand the ruse but don't have time to object, as the nurse walks in and sees me fussing with the glasses. She confiscates them. "You can't wear those during surgery."

As we wait outside the operating room, Jade reaches over and switches the elastic bands that designate me as the donor and her as the recipient.

The head surgical nurse appears and makes sure the donor and the recipient are properly tagged. Before the anesthesiologist arrives, it is discovered that our different-colored gowns are reversed. The change is quickly made to coincide with the wrist bands. At least to the surgeons, it will be clear that Jade is the donor and that I am the recipient.

PART NINE

A NEW BEGINNING

JADE N/K/A CRIMSON

THE OFFICIAL TIME OF DEATH was listed as one-eighteen p.m., November 11, 2011. The official cause of death was listed as death by lethal injection. Her body was released and she was buried in the family plot next to her brother and parents. To confirm that the body was that of Crimson Ziang, the county coroner had checked not only the identifying mark, a yin-yang tattoo on the right ankle, but compared the photograph of the face of the corpse with that of the mug shot that was on file. It was unclear whether the coroner did any DNA testing. It was obvious no one had checked the fingerprints.

When the condemned had been brought into the execution chamber that November day, she was allowed to take with her the gold diamond-studded cross Dora Duquesne had given her in anticipation of her impending kidney transplant. Though Dora never told her of its miraculous powers, she believed. She knew that where she was headed from here was in the hands of him who gives everlasting life. She also knew that her future had been scripted since the beginning of time. She just didn't know what it was and, if the truth was known, neither did the author of this novel.

CRIMSON N/K/A JADE

AS THE PATIENT WAS RECOVERING from her surgery, she was told she had a surprise visitor. It was Adrien. He had flown from Paris to San Francisco to be with his wife. Adrien later told the doctor that he was concerned about his wife because she was disoriented and didn't appear to recognize him. Adrien was told not to worry, that that was just the effects of surgery and the heavy sedation. She was doing just fine and would be her old self before long.

Crimson played the role she was now cast in. She was no longer Crimson but Jade and would remain so the rest of her life. She faked much of it very well and what she couldn't fake she blamed on amnesia. Even Adrien relished in his role as caregiver in the rehabilitation phase. For both it was an exploration process that made life intriguing and exciting once again. Adrien would later tell Jacques that it was like being on a second honeymoon.

Even with all the hints that surrounded her upon her return to France, Jade's amnestic condition failed to improve. In fact, it was more pronounced than ever. She had to revert to English and it was as if she never had been exposed to the French language, or so it seemed when she stumbled as she attempted to comprehend and speak it. Her condition prevented her from performing her usual functions at RMC and she was ultimately placed on indefinite leave.

Back in the States and with the assistance of an attorney, Jade was able to persuade the probate judge assigned to her parents' estate to terminate the trust and place all the assets in her name. Since the income beneficiaries were now deceased and the estate income was then becoming part of the principal, it would ultimately revert to the benefit of the contin-gent beneficiary of the trust corpus anyway, which was her.

Adrien had always wanted to live in the United States and this was now his chance. Although he did not particularly relish leaving behind his sister and a relatively lucrative job, he was looking forward to the opportunities America presented.

So, on that breezy March day, 2012, the Jardines arrived at the San Francisco International Airport with little more than a few suitcases. There, they were met by Rachel and Miles Josselyn who transported them to the old family mansion near Golden Gate National Recreational Area overlooking South Bay and the Pacific Ocean. As between Rachel and Jade, it would be like old times. "It was the same old Jade in looks but not personality," Rachel would later tell Miles. "With a new kidney and a new outlook on life, Jade was more like Crimson than her old self."

"Not a bad thing," Miles would add. "After all, Crimson is now a part of her." The profundity of his statement would be appreciated only by the person of whom the two spoke.

PART TEN

REVERSING
THE CURSE

CRIMSON N/K/A JADE

AS ADRIEN TOOK OVER the management of Chi-Yen's and Jade the family enterprises, they grew closer and marveled at how dis*appointment*, deva*station* and dis*grace* could in such a short period of time be transformed into a divine *appointment*, envied *station* in life and state of *grace*.

While Adrien and Jade relaxed in the quiet of the night and gazed at the star-filled sky above San Francisco, they observed a bright star appear from nowhere and hover over them like a spotlight. Then a second star in close proximity and then a third. The three luminaries seemed to dance as if to some kind of mysterious rhythm and then disappear.

"Did you see that?" Adrien asked as he sat in bewilderment.

"Yes," Jade responded. "And I could see the smiling faces of my mother, father and brother."

Just then they saw another star separate from the vast cluster, even more radiant than the previous three. It appeared, danced and then disappeared.

"Crimson!" Adrien said.

"Yes, Crimson," Jade said. "I notice you didn't make that a question."

"I saw her face, too," Adrien said. "And," he added, "it wasn't frowning."

Jade thought back to their first day at the beach shortly after their arrival in San Francisco. She remembered the sun shining in such a way as to highlight the tattoo on her right ankle. She saw the quizzical look on Adrien's face as he viewed it. He never said anything at the time but he remained quiet and said little for an agonizing period of time. She wondered what he was thinking. Her curiosity was getting the better of her.

Mustering up the courage, she now asked, "Honey, remember that first day at the beach and we had just returned from a quick dip in the Pacific?"

"Yes."

"Was that not a special time?"

"Yes, why do you ask?"

"You seemed preoccupied at the time by my tattoo and yet said nothing. Was there something about my tattoo that troubled you?"

"I was wondering how it was that the patterns were reversed and the dark pattern appeared last. Then it occurred to me that your curse had been reversed and that your life had been turned around as a result of your kidney transplant. If I hadn't known better I would have thought you had had a heart transplant."

"Are you saying that with the white pattern appearing first you consider me lily-white?"

"Yes, and innocent, too."

"Don't exaggerate. I may be *innocent* but not *lily-white*. There are various shades of innocence but none *lily-white*."

ABOUT THE AUTHOR

Carroll Multz has authored or co-authored thirteen books and technical manuals. This is his sixth novel. A trial lawyer for over forty years, a former two-term district attorney, assistant attorney general, and judge, he has been involved in cases ranging from municipal courts to and including the United States Supreme Court. Multz's high profile cases have been reported in the *New York Times, Redbook Magazine* and various police magazines. He was one of the attorneys in the Columbine Copycat Case that occurred in Fort Collins, Colorado, in 2001 that was featured by Barbara Walters on ABC's *20/20*. Now retired, Multz is an Adjunct Professor at Colorado Mesa University in Grand Junction, Colorado, teaching law-related courses at both the graduate and undergraduate levels.